# THE BOND MARKET IN THE REPUBLIC OF KOREA
## AN ASEAN+3 BOND MARKET GUIDE UPDATE

MAY 2024

ADB

ASIAN DEVELOPMENT BANK

© 2024 Asian Development Bank
6 ADB Avenue, Mandaluyong City, 1550 Metro Manila, Philippines
Tel +63 2 8632 4444; Fax +63 2 8636 2444
www.adb.org

Some rights reserved. Published in 2024.

ISBN 978-92-9270-684-5 (print), 978-92-9270-685-2 (PDF), 978-92-9270-686-9 (ebook)
ISSN 2616-4663 (print), 2616-4671 (PDF)
Publication Stock No. TCS240245-2
DOI: http://dx.doi.org/10.22617/TCS240245-2

Notes:
In this publication, international standards for naming conventions—International Organization for Standardization (ISO) 3166 for economy codes and ISO 4217 for currency codes—are used to reflect the discussions of the ASEAN+3 Bond Market Forum to promote and support implementation of international standards in financial transactions in the region. ASEAN+3 comprises the Association of Southeast Asian Nations (ASEAN) plus the People's Republic of China, Japan, and the Republic of Korea.

The economies of ASEAN+3 as defined in ISO 3166 include Brunei Darussalam (BN; BRN); Cambodia (KH; KHM); the People's Republic of China (CN; CHN); Hong Kong, China (HK; HKG); Indonesia (ID; IDN); Japan (JP; JPN); the Republic of Korea (KR; KOR); the Lao People's Democratic Republic (LA; LAO); Malaysia (MY; MYS); the Philippines (PH; PHL); Singapore (SG; SGP); Thailand (TH; THA); and Viet Nam (VN; VNM).

The currencies of ASEAN+3 as defined in ISO 4217 include the Brunei dollar (BND), Cambodian riel (KHR), Chinese renminbi (CNY), Hong Kong dollar (HKD), Indonesian rupiah (IDR), Japanese yen (JPY), Korean won (KRW), Lao kip (LAK), Malaysian ringgit (MYR), Philippine peso (PHP), Singapore dollar (SGD), Thai baht (THB), and Vietnamese dong (VND).

ADB recognizes "Hongkong" and "Hong Kong" as Hong Kong, China; "Korea" and "S. Korea" as the Republic of Korea; and "Korean" as referring to the Republic of Korea.

# Contents

Note: The chapter and section numbering reflect that of *the ASEAN+3 Bond Market Guide Republic of Korea 2018* and includes only the chapters and sections being updated.

# Tables and Figures

# Acknowledgments

The *ASEAN+3 Bond Market Guide Republic of Korea* was published in May 2018.[1] Since then, and particularly given recent announcements, the Korean bond market has undergone significant change as part of larger reforms in the Korean capital market. As such, an update of the original *ASEAN+3 Bond Market Guide Republic of Korea* has become necessary.[2]

This update note was compiled by Shigehito Inukai and Matthias Schmidt, Asian Development Bank (ADB) consultants, with significant contributions from Jiwoong Choi and Eunjae Shin, financial sector specialists in the Economic Research and Development Impact Department of ADB.

The ASEAN+3 Bond Market Forum (ABMF) team wishes to thank the Bank of Korea, the Financial Services Commission and Financial Supervisory Service, Korea Exchange, the Korea Financial Investment Association, as well as the Korea Securities Depository and ABMF International Experts, particularly Citibank Korea Inc., Deutsche Bank AG Seoul Branch, and the Hongkong and Shanghai Banking Corporation Seoul Branch for their inputs and review of this update note. Special thanks go to the Ministry of Economy and Finance of the Republic of Korea for its strong support.

In addition, the ABMF team acknowledges inputs from Leelark Park, former ADB consultant; Joong Shik Lee, ADB consultant; as well as Korean bond market participants that are not ABMF members, including Kookmin Bank, who contributed their time and expertise in support of this update note.

No part of this update note represents the official views or opinions of any institution that participated in this activity as an ABMF member, observer, or expert. The ABMF Sub-Forum 1 team bears sole responsibility for the contents of this update note.

This update note and those relating to other ASEAN+3 bond markets are available for download from *AsianBondsOnline*.[3]

May 2024

ASEAN+3 Bond Market Forum

---

[1] ADB. 2018. *ASEAN+3 Bond Market Guide Republic of Korea*. Manila. https://asianbondsonline.adb.org/abmg.php#kor-2018.

[2] ASEAN+3 comprises the Association of Southeast Asian Nations (ASEAN) plus the People's Republic of China, Japan, and the Republic of Korea.

[3] AsianBondsOnline. https://asianbondsonline.adb.org.

# Abbreviations

| | |
|---|---|
| ABMF | ASEAN+3 Bond Market Forum |
| ADB | Asian Development Bank |
| ASEAN | Association of Southeast Asian Nations |
| ASEAN+3 | ASEAN plus the People's Republic of China, Japan, and the Republic of Korea |
| BOK | Bank of Korea |
| CD | certificate of deposit |
| CD91 | certificate of deposit with 91-day tenor |
| COVID-19 | coronavirus disease |
| ESG | environmental, social, and (corporate) governance principles |
| FSC | Financial Services Commission |
| FSCMA | Financial Investment Services and Capital Markets Act |
| FSS | Financial Supervisory Service |
| FX | foreign exchange |
| GDP | gross domestic product |
| ICSD | international central securities depository |
| ICMA | International Capital Market Association |
| IRC | Investor Registration Certificate |
| KCMI | Korea Capital Market Institute |
| KOFIA | Korea Financial Investment Association |
| KOFR | Korea Overnight Financing Repo Rate |
| KOSPI | Korea Composite Stock Price Index |
| KRW | Korean won (ISO code) |
| KRX | Korea Exchange |
| KSD | Korea Securities Depository |
| KTB | Korea Treasury Bond |
| KTBi | Korea Treasury Bond (inflation-linked) |
| KYC | know your customer |
| K-GBG | Korea Green Bond Guidelines |
| LEI | Legal Entity Identifier |
| LCY | local currency |
| LIBOR | London Interbank Offered Rate |
| MOE | Ministry of Environment |
| MOEF | Ministry of Economy and Finance |
| MOJ | Ministry of Justice |
| MSB | Monetary Stabilization Bond |
| NTS | National Tax Service |
| OTC | over-the-counter |

QFI        Qualified Foreign Intermediary
QIB        Qualified Institutional Buyer
RFI        Registered Foreign Institution
SRI        socially responsible investment (bonds)
SRO        self-regulatory organization
USD        United States dollar (ISO code)

USD1 = KRW1,346.80 as of 29 March 2024
(official rate from Seoul Money Brokerage)

# Overview

## A.  Introduction

The bond market in the Republic of Korea is undergoing significant changes as part of larger reforms in the Korean capital market. Policymakers and regulatory authorities recognized the need to make the Korean market more investor-friendly overall and more accessible to foreign investors by addressing identified issues and weaknesses with a set of policy measures announced as far back as 2022—a move seen as favorable in view of the expected inclusion of Korean government bonds in international bond indices in the coming years. Quite a number of these changes will have been implemented by the time of publication of this update note, with other measures being phased into the market over the next few years. This update note offers information on those changes in the context of the structure of the original *ASEAN+3 Bond Market Guide Republic of Korea*, with only relevant sections being displayed here.

Most notably, the Government of the Republic of Korea abolished the need for new foreign investors to obtain an Investor Registration Certificate (IRC) in late 2023, a practice that had been in place for nearly 3 decades but was often seen as a hurdle to market entry even if the actual process had become fairly straightforward in recent years. Chapter II.K offers a detailed description of the new market entry process using the Legal Entity Identifier (LEI).

Policy measures for improved market access also included a liberalization of the foreign exchange (FX) market, with investors now able to conduct FX transactions with a third party or register to become a direct market participant (see details in Chapter II.M).

Other measures already implemented include the exemption of withholding tax for foreign investors on interest stemming from Korea Treasury Bonds (KTBs) and Monetary Stabilization Bonds (MSBs), as is explained in Chapter VI.H, and the introduction of an indirect market access option for foreign bond investors via international central securities depositories' (ICSDs) use of an omnibus account; details on the latter are available in Chapter II.K and II.M.

Ongoing and very recent changes relate to the improvement of disclosure in English (see Chapter II.G) and the introduction of long-term KTB futures contracts on Korea Exchange (KRX); details on the latter are available in Chapter IV.J.

On the legislative side, the introduction of the Electronic Securities Act in 2019 and its subsidiary regulations, to cement the drive toward a dematerialized securities market, is also laying the foundation for a formal definition of digital assets and the formulation of a digital asset framework and related products, enabling fintech innovation and the use of resultant big data. Policymakers are expected to promulgate a dedicated law, while intending to amend existing laws and regulations in line with international best practice (see details in

Chapter II.C). The impact of the Electronic Securities Act, 2019 on both market actors and practices is explained in a number of different sections of this update note.[4]

In parallel with the above features, the Korean market has also been very prolific in the introduction of sustainable finance instruments in line with global developments. Since 2018, when the Korea Development Bank issued both the first green bond and social bond in the domestic market, the issuance volume and variety of sustainable finance instruments—the typical technical terms used in the Korean market are either "socially responsible investment (SRI) bonds" or "environmental, social, and (corporate) governance (ESG) bonds"—has grown significantly in the Korean market. At the same time, the Government of the Republic of Korea and Korean corporates have also tapped international bond markets for sustainable finance instruments to great effect. Supporting this development is the so-called "K-Taxonomy" and related guidelines, a policy framework that defines SRI and ESG activities, and also offers incentives to issuers of such bonds, as explained in Chapter III.B and other sections.

**Figure 1.1: Local Currency Bonds Outstanding in the Republic of Korea, 2018–2023 (USD billion)**

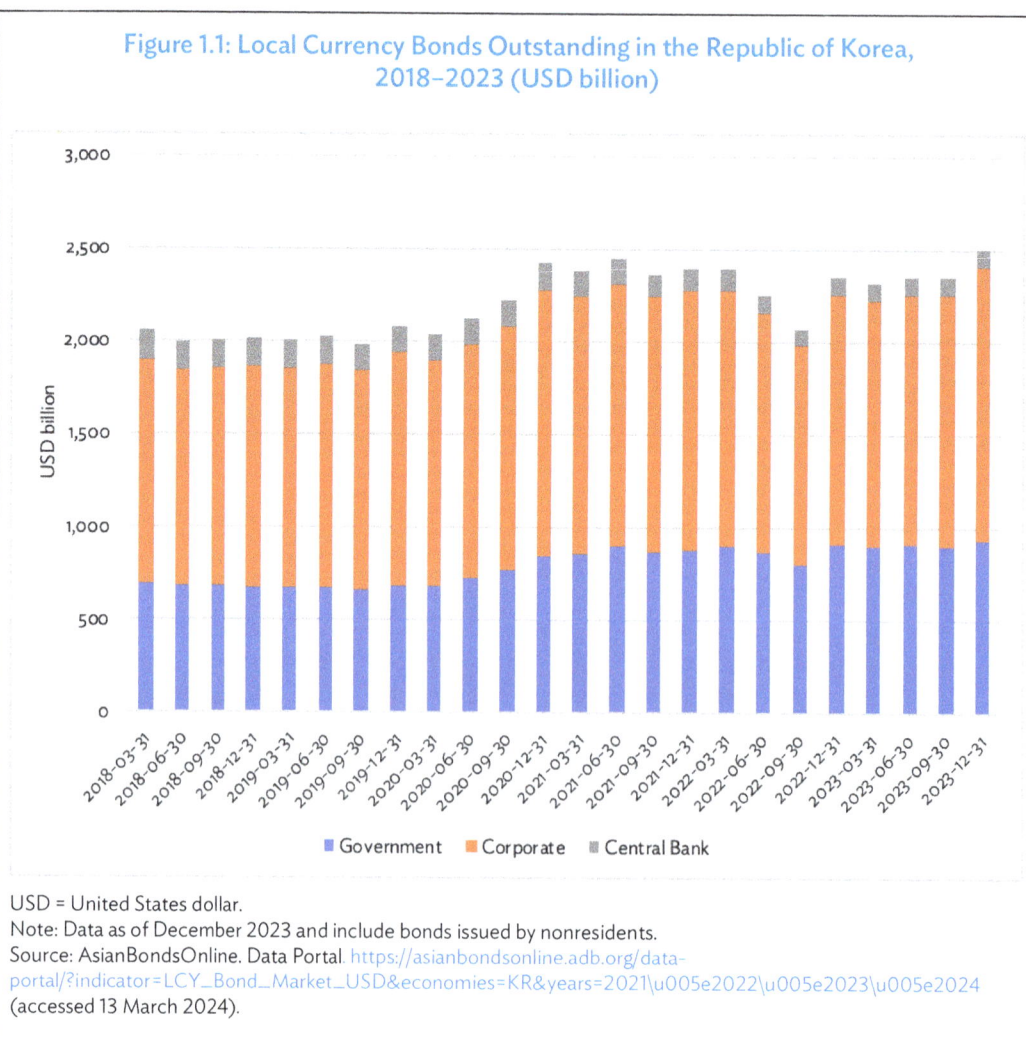

USD = United States dollar.
Note: Data as of December 2023 and include bonds issued by nonresidents.
Source: AsianBondsOnline. Data Portal. https://asianbondsonline.adb.org/data-portal/?indicator=LCY_Bond_Market_USD&economies=KR&years=2021\u005e2022\u005e2023\u005e2024 (accessed 13 March 2024).

---

[4] The Electronic Securities Act, 2019 (official name: Act Concerning Electronic Registration of Stocks/Bonds, etc.) was ratified by the National Assembly in 2016, but only became effective on 16 September 2019, after a period of deliberation about the act's enforcement decree. The text of the act is available in English from the Korea Law Translation Center at https://elaw.klri.re.kr/eng_mobile/viewer.do?hseq=38455&type=new&key=.

While the Korean bond market's size remained relatively stable in local currency (LCY) terms over the 3-year period ending in 2023, if measured in US dollar terms (**Figure 1.1**), the market posted a growth of 21.5% compared to the beginning of 2018, the year in which the original *ASEAN+3 Bond Market Guide Republic of Korea* was published. The amount of bonds outstanding expanded on increased KTB issuance in 2020 and 2021 in response to the fiscal impact of the coronavirus disease (COVID-19), before holding relatively steady in both 2022 and 2023. If measured in LCY terms, the overall growth of the domestic bond market from 2018 to 2023 amounted to 47.0% (**Figure 1.2**).

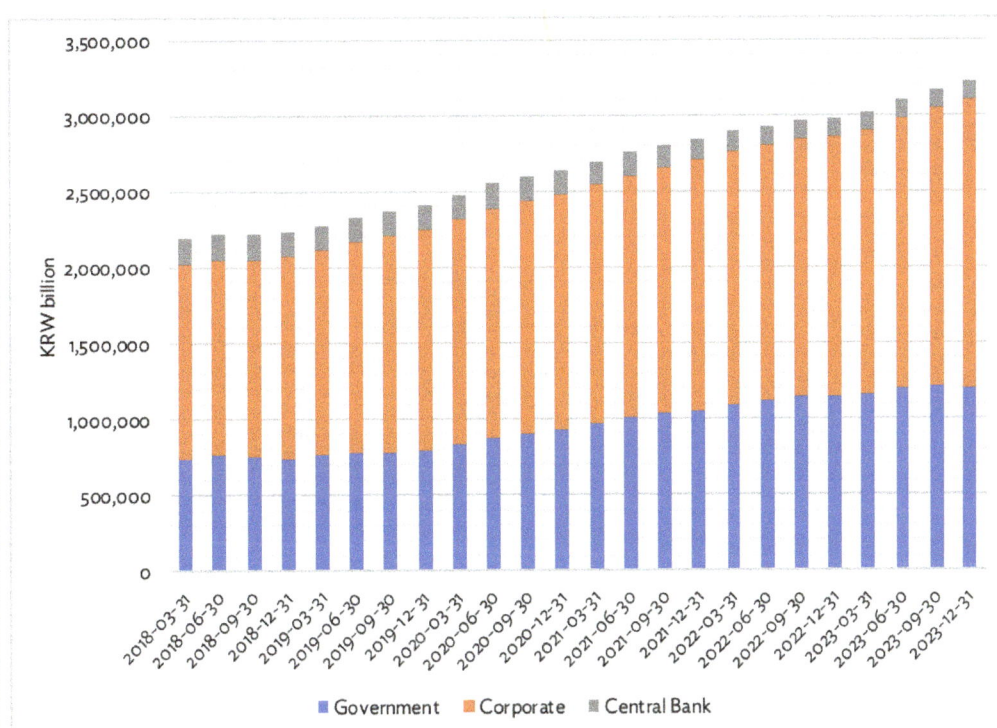

Figure 1.2: Local Currency Bonds Outstanding in the Republic of Korea, 2018–2023 (KRW billion)

KRW = Korean won.
Note: Data as of December 2023 and include bonds issued by nonresidents.
Source: AsianBondsOnline. Data Portal. https://asianbondsonline.adb.org/data-portal/?indicator=LCY_Bond_Market_USD&economies=KR&years=2021\u005e2022\u005e2023\u005e2024 (accessed 13 March 2024).

The Korean LCY bond market as a whole is of significant size when compared to other regional bond markets and selected markets overseas, particularly when measured in relation to gross domestic product (GDP) (**Figure 1.3**).

**Figure 1.3: The Republic of Korea's Local Currency Bond Market Size versus Selected Markets (% of GDP)**

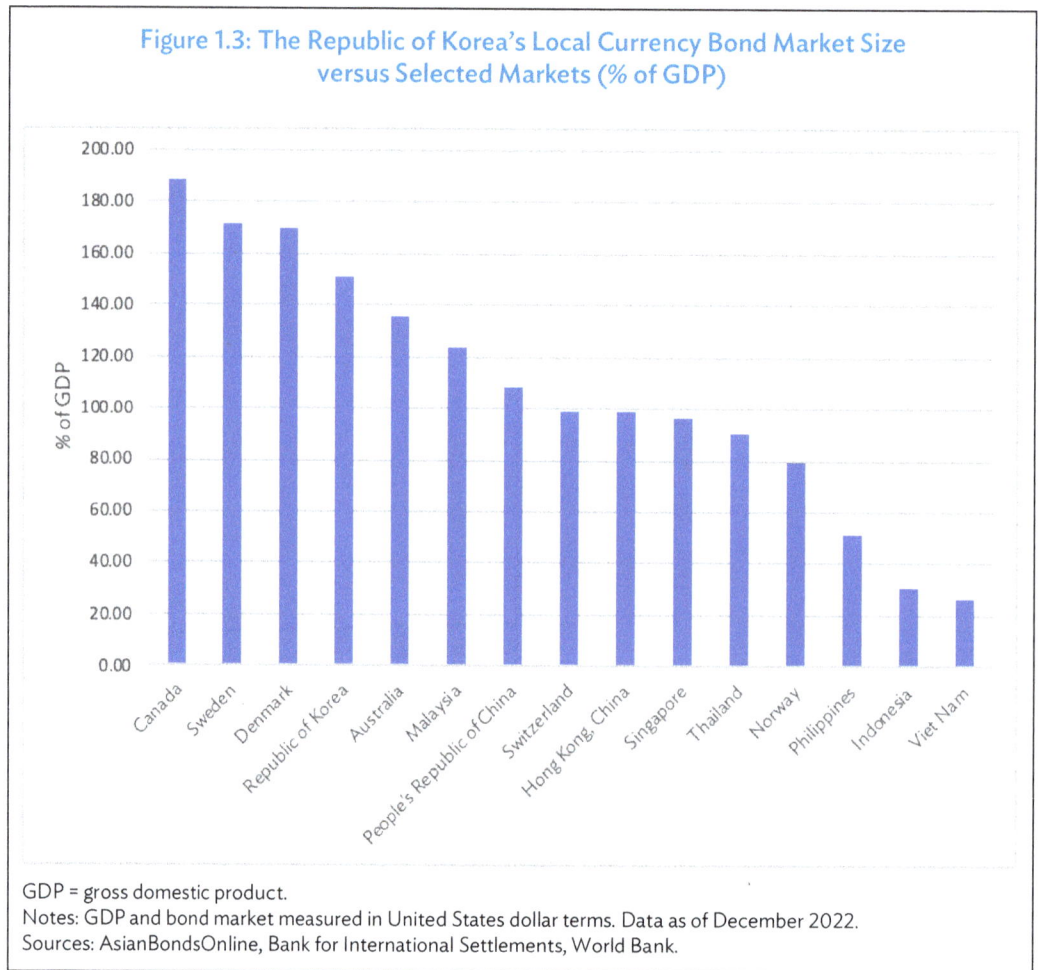

GDP = gross domestic product.
Notes: GDP and bond market measured in United States dollar terms. Data as of December 2022.
Sources: AsianBondsOnline, Bank for International Settlements, World Bank.

The chart shows that the Korean LCY bond market is significantly bigger, as a share of GDP, than many other LCY bond markets in the region. It is also larger than established bond markets in some major economies around the world.

It is envisaged that the follow-on effect from the abovementioned policy measures and those still to come, including the likely inclusion of Korean government bonds in international bond indices, will be beneficial for the further growth and segmentation of the Korean bond market and the capital market overall.

# Legal and Regulatory Framework

This chapter reviews the significant changes or updates to rules and regulations, regulatory processes, and other official prescriptions by regulatory authorities and market institutions in the Korean bond and capital markets since the publication of the *ASEAN+3 Bond Market Guide Republic of Korea.* The structure follows the original bond market guide, and only sections with updates or corrections are shown in each chapter; new subjects are added at the end of existing sections and are marked accordingly.

## C.    Legislative Structure

A number of new laws, regulations, and rules with relevance for the bond market have been promulgated or introduced in the Republic of Korea since the publication of the original bond market guide in 2018, while much of the key and fundamental legislation and regulations for the bond market have been revised in the intervening years. In turn, some laws and regulations have been rescinded. **Table 2.1** has been updated accordingly for easy reference.

While the new laws and regulations will be referenced or reviewed in detail in the relevant chapters and sections of this update note, established and since revised laws and regulations are shown in the table if they are also referenced in this publication and marked "New" if they appear in the table for the first time. Table entries are presented in reverse chronological order.

Table 2.1: Examples of Securities Market Legislation and Regulations by Legislative Tier

| Legislative Tier | Contents or Significant Examples |
|---|---|
| Constitution of the Republic of Korea (1988) | Principles, Rights, and Obligations |
| Statutes and acts (fundamental and key legislation for the market and market participants) | <ul><li>Act on the Protection of Virtual Asset Users (effective 1 July 2024) [New]</li><li>Financial Investment Services and Capital Markets Act (revised 22 September 2023)</li><li>Act on the Establishment, etc. of the Financial Services Commission (revised 14 September 2023)</li><li>Corporate Tax Act (revised 1 July 2023) [New]</li><li>Income Tax Act (revised 1 July 2023)</li><li>Foreign Exchange Transaction Act (revised 16 September 2021)</li><li>Environmental Technology and Industry Support Act (revised 21 April 2021)</li></ul> |

*continued on next page*

Table 2.1 *continued*

- Act on the Management of Financial Benchmarks of the Republic of Korea (promulgated 26 November 2019, effective 24 November 2020) [New]
- Act on Electronic Registration of Stocks, Bonds, etc. (promulgated 22 March 2016, effective 16 September 2019) [New]
- The Bank of Korea Act (Revised 13 March 2018)

| | |
|---|---|
| Subsidiary legislation (Presidential Decree or Enforcement Rule of the prime minister or relevant ministry) | • Enforcement Decree of the Foreign Exchange Transaction Act (revised 4 October 2023)<br>• Enforcement Decree of the Banking Act (revised 22 September 2023)<br>• Enforcement Decree of the Corporate Tax Act (23 September 2023)<br>• Enforcement Decree of the Income Tax Act (1 October 2023)<br>• Enforcement Decree of the Act on Electronic Registration of Stocks, Bonds, etc. (16 September 2019) [New]<br><br>Financial Services Commission (FSC)<br>• FSC Regulation on Financial Investment Business (revised 22 December 2023)<br>• FSC Regulation on Issuance, Public Disclosure, etc. of Securities (revised 1 May 2023)<br>• FSC–MOJ Regulation on Authorization, etc. for Electronic Registration Business (September 2019) [New]<br>• FSC Regulation on Electronic Registration Business (16 September 2019) [New]<br>• Enforcement Decree of the Financial Investment Services and Capital Markets Act (revised 14 December 2023)<br><br>Financial Supervisory Service (FSS)<br>• FSS Detailed Rules of the Regulation on Financial Investment Business (revised 14 December 2023)<br>• FSS Detailed Regulations on Issuance, Public Disclosure, etc. of Securities (revised 12 April 2021) |
| Self-regulatory organization rules (e.g., from KOFIA or KRX, and their enforcement rules) | Korea Exchange (KRX)<br>• KOSPI Market Business Regulation (revised 19 July 2023)<br>• KOSPI Market Disclosure Regulation (revised 29 March 2023)<br>• KOSPI Market Listing Regulation (revised 7 December 2022)<br>• Guidelines for Operation of Segment Dedicated to Socially Responsible Investment Bonds (December 2019) [New]<br><br>Korea Financial Investment Association (KOFIA)<br>• Regulations on Securities Underwriting Business, etc. (revised 8 June 2023)<br>• Guidelines on ESG Bonds Ratings (January 2023) [New]<br>• Regulations on Registration and Management, etc. of Securities for Qualified Institutional Buyers (revised 21 August 2018)<br><br>Korea Securities Depository<br>• Regulation on Deposit Service for Securities (revised 24 November 2021)<br>• Securities Lending and Borrowing Regulation (revised 24 November 2021)<br>• Regulation of Electronic Registration Services for Stocks, Bonds, etc. (8 March 2021) [New]<br>• Regulation on Settlement Service for Securities (revised 28 August 2019)<br>• Regulation on Bond Registration Business (revised 16 August 2019) |

ESG = environmental, social, and governance; KOSPI = Korea Composite Stock Price Index; MOJ = Ministry of Justice.
Note: In the Korean bond market, the term "enforcement" in the context of laws and regulations can have multiple meanings; it is typically used to denote the effective date of a law or regulation, or an implementation decree, and may not describe a response to a regulation or rule violation, as may be expected in other markets.
Source: ASEAN+3 Bond Market Forum (ABMF) and ABMF constituents.

### 1.    Fundamental and Key Legislation (Statutes and Acts)

The Government of the Republic of Korea announced an exemption from withholding tax on KTBs and MSBs for foreign investors, effective 1 January 2023. To provide the legal basis for the tax exemption, the Ministry of Economy and Finance (MOEF) revised in 2023 the Income Tax Act and Corporate Tax Act, as well as the respective enforcement decrees of these two acts, while granting a zero-rating to the withholding tax between the effective date and the law's change.

A key addition to the legal and regulatory framework for the bond market in the Republic of Korea has been the introduction of the Act on Electronic Registration of Stocks, Bonds, etc (i.e., the Electronic Securities Act, 2019). While market authorities had made efforts to immobilize physical securities many years ago and select instrument types had been limited to electronic issuance, the Electronic Securities Act, 2019 enshrined the concept that securities such as listed bonds, special bonds such as equity-linked bonds and contingent-convertible bonds, and mortgage-backed securities are required to be issued and circulated only as electronic records. The act and its subsidiary decree took effect on 16 September 2019.

The Electronic Securities Act, 2019 is considered a necessary precursor to any policy measures or legislation related to digital assets, as is the Act on the Protection of Virtual Asset Users (effective 1 July 2024). The latter is intended to protect the rights and interests of virtual asset users and promote the establishment of fair, transparent, and sound trading practices in the virtual asset markets. A more detailed description of the activities under the Electronic Securities Act can be found in Chapter III.I, while the subject of digital assets is mentioned in Chapter III.B.

Also, newly included in the list of statutes and acts are the (i) Foreign Exchange Transaction Act, widely known as FETA, due to recent liberalization measures in the FX market; and (ii) Environmental Technology and Industry Support Act (as amended in 2021), which gave the Ministry of Environment (MOE) the legal basis to formulate its K-Taxonomy, subsidiary regulations, and industry guidance. See Chapter III.B for the relevance of the K-Taxonomy.

One additional significant development was the promulgation of the Act on the Management of Financial Benchmarks of the Republic of Korea in November 2019 (effective 24 November 2020) as a policy response to the discontinuation of the London Interbank Offered Rate (LIBOR) as an internationally utilized reference rate. This development is referenced in Chapter X.A, with further details provided in Chapter IV.K.

### 2.    Subsidiary Legislation (Decrees or Enforcement Rules)

Subsidiary legislation and regulations related to the Electronic Securities Act, 2019 include the Enforcement Decree of the Act on Electronic Registration of Stocks, Bonds, etc.; the Financial Services Commission–Ministry of Justice (FSC–MOJ) Regulation on Authorization, etc. for Electronic Registration Business; and the FSC Regulation on Electronic Registration Business. In addition, various fundamental laws such as the Financial Investment Services and Capital Market Act, Banking Act, and Commercial Act, as well as subsidiary regulations, were revised to reflect the concept of electronic securities and remain consistent with the Electronic Securities Act, 2019. Under the electronic securities system, information about ownership and the transfer of securities rights—in this context, the legal rights associated with the ownership of the securities including entitlements—are recorded electronically, which will help eliminate the risk of theft or counterfeit securities and aid in the prevention of tax evasion.

Significant policy measures, such as the abolition of the IRC and the reactivation of an omnibus account option for foreign investors, which in principle already existed in the subsidiary legislation of the Financial Investment Services and Capital Market Act (FSCMA), led to a revision of the Enforcement Decree of the FSCMA; the revisions bill of the FSCMA was approved on 5 June 2023 and became effective on 14 December 2023, though the effective dates for both measures may differ. For more information on the IRC's abolition and the indirect market access option afforded by the omnibus account, please refer to section K in this chapter.

### 3.    Self-Regulatory Organization Rules

The Electronic Securities Act, 2019 affirmed the Korea Securities Depository (KSD) as the official electronic registry. In turn, KSD established its Regulation on the Electronic Registration Services for Stock, Bonds, etc. and revised existing regulations such as the Regulation on Settlement Service for Securities, the Regulation on Deposit Service for Securities, the Regulation on Bond Registration Business, and the Securities Lending and Borrowing Regulation to provide electronic registration and related services to securities issuers, underwriters, and investors. In contrast to past KSD regulations, any new (or changes to existing) regulations in relation to the Electronic Securities Act, 2019 will require the prior approval of the MOJ, in addition to the FSC.

In addition to regular revisions of its market business, disclosure, and listing rules (see section J in this chapter for details), KRX also issued the Guidelines for Operation of Segment Dedicated to Socially Responsible Investment Bonds in December 2019 to guide market participants and interested parties on the SRI-specific website operated by KRX.[5]

## D.    Korean Bond Market Regulatory Structure

While the regulatory structure of the bond market has not changed in principle since the publication of the *ASEAN+3 Bond Market Guide Republic of Korea*, the MOE and the MOJ have assumed additional roles in relation to sustainable finance instruments and the review and promulgation of certain regulations, respectively. These additional roles are described below. For the roles of other regulatory authorities, market institutions, and self-regulatory organizations (SROs), please refer to the original publication.

### 1.    Ministry of Economy and Finance

The Ministry of Strategy and Finance was renamed the Ministry of Economy and Finance (MOEF), effective 1 August 2018, following a review by the Advisory Committee on English Names of Government Organizations. The name change was intended to better reflect its role of governing the overall economic and fiscal policies in the Republic of Korea to the international community. However, the remit of the MOEF has not changed, including and in particular in relation to the bond market in the Republic of Korea.

### 5.    Korea Financial Investment Association

As a correction to the previous description of Korea Financial Investment Association's (KOFIA) self-regulatory powers in the *ASEAN+3 Bond Market Guide Republic of Korea*, it should be stated that in the case of a violation of KOFIA rules by a member company, KOFIA's Self-Regulation Committee can assess the violation and recommend a penalty on the member. However, the penalty would be imposed and enforced by either the FSC or the Financial Supervisory Service (FSS) under powers delegated by the FSC, as the case may be.

---

[5] The guidelines are available from Korea Exchange at https://sribond.krx.co.kr/en/index.jsp.

### 8.    Ministry of Environment [New]

The MOE was established in January 1990 under the Office of the Prime Minister and given greater authority to establish and implement its own policies in 1994. In line with the "Green New Deal" Initiative, the MOE introduced measures to establish a foundation for green industry growth, such as preparing a Korean-style green finance classification system and a guide to green bonds in 2020, taking its cues from the European Union's decision to introduce a "sustainable financial strategy" and plan to establish an international sustainable finance platform.[6]

In April 2021, the Environmental Technology and Industry Support Act was passed by the National Assembly, on the basis of which the MOE established a national green taxonomy. This K-Taxonomy refers to the classification of green economic activities contributing to six environmental goals: (i) greenhouse gas reduction, (ii) adaptation to climate change, (iii) sustainable water conservation, (iv) recycling, (v) pollution prevention, and (vi) management and biodiversity.

To provide more detailed and practical information for market participants and other stakeholders, the MOE issued the K-Taxonomy Guidelines in December 2021. While the guidelines are not legally binding, they provide principles and standards on which economic activities can be regarded as green activities, thereby assisting in the allocation of funds to green economic activities, including projects and technologies.

Please see Chapter III.B for a description of sustainable finance instruments as a result of the use of the K-Taxonomy and its related guidelines.

### 9.    Ministry of Justice [New]

In relation to the bond market, the MOJ had traditionally enabled the issuance of corporate bonds through relevant provisions in the Commercial Act, which it continues to administer. With the introduction of the Electronic Securities Act in September 2019, the MOJ emerged as the main government authority in standards- and procedure-setting for the electronic securities system; the MOJ now regulates the electronic registry, securities issuing companies, account management institutions, and other stakeholders in relation to the electronic securities system, in conjunction with the FSC.

## E.    Regulatory Framework for Debt Securities

Given that two new ministries have been added as regulatory stakeholders—and with new legislation, regulations, and rules in place—this section aims to briefly restate the regulatory framework for the Korean bond market, including any necessary corrections.

---

[6] The Green New Deal, announced by the MOE in July 2020 as part of the government's so-called "Korean New Deal," represents the strategy to lead the Republic of Korea toward a low-carbon economy and away from a carbon-based industrial ecosystem. As part of the Green New Deal, policymakers have implemented protective measures for people and sectors that can be marginalized during the economic and social transitions. A booklet in English on the Korean New Deal and its component policies is available for download from the MOEF website at https://english.moef.go.kr/pc/selectTbPressCenterDtl.do?boardCd=N0001&seq=4948%20.

### 1.   General Regulatory Framework

In the case of a public offering of debt securities, a registration of the proposed issuance with the FSC is required. In contrast, private placements other than those offerings in the Qualified Institutional Buyer (QIB) market are issued in the market through negotiation between the issuer and underwriters. Once the debt securities are issued, applicable regulations are largely dependent on whether the securities are traded on the exchange or in the over-the-counter (OTC) market. Exchange trading is regulated by FSC, FSS, and KRX rules; only publicly offered bonds can be listed on the exchange. Trading in the OTC market, which is possible for both publicly offered and privately placed bonds and notes, is regulated by the FSC and FSS, with KOFIA acting as the SRO for the OTC market.

The MOEF represents the issuer of government bonds, with the Bank of Korea (BOK) acting as issuing agent and setting the practices for auction and the primary market. The MOJ does not play a direct role in the issuance, listing, trading, or transfer of debt securities, but it does review and must approve participating institutions in relation to the electronic securities system.

## G.   Continuous Disclosure Requirements in the Korean Bond Market

One of the major policy changes in recent years in the Korean capital market concerns the introduction of mandatory disclosure in English for companies that have their stocks listed on the Korea Composite Stock Price Index (KOSPI) market (main board) of KRX. The new disclosure obligation applies to information for all securities issued by KOSPI-listed companies, including both listed and unlisted bonds. Corporates who only have bonds listed on KRX are not affected by this new policy (see Public Offers below).

This measure affects both the initial and the continuous disclosure practices in the market; and it is expected to support the policy objective to make the overall Korean capital market more accessible to foreign investors. In 2022, the FSS observed that only 13.8% of all company disclosure information submitted to it was also made available in English, a level considered insufficient and not in line with the practices in major advanced economies, including those in Asia. In addition, any English information that was submitted to the FSS was typically the result of a machine-translation process, generally limited to the financial statements, which can lead to the ambiguous or misleading use of terms.

To ease issuers into the additional disclosure obligation, policymakers have set a phased approach, with the starting date of January 2024 applying initially only to large corporates (classified as those with assets of KRW10 trillion or more) listed on the KOSPI market and corporates with assets of more than KRW2 trillion that have foreign shareholding of 30% or more. This is in recognition that companies of that size likely have issued securities in international markets where English disclosure already prevails. Disclosures in English are to be made available within 3 days from the information being published in Korean. From 2026, the obligation will be expanded to corporates with assets of KRW2 trillion or more, while English disclosure for large companies is expected when any disclosure in Korean is made.

The disclosure obligations itself follow the existing statutory requirements set out in the FSCMA (Article 391: Disclosure Regulations), relevant regulations, and KRX listing and disclosure rules, but they have a particular focus on any disclosure in relation to the financial position of a company, including the provision of financial statements, and on material events affecting the issuer as well as any information relating to trading halts or resumptions. As is the practice in the Republic of Korea, the statutory places of disclosure are both the FSS and KRX under their respective regulations and rules; information sent to the Data

Analysis, Retrieval, and Transfer System (DART), the official corporate filing repository in the Republic Korea operated by the FSS, is accessible to the public at large via a dedicated website and is also available in English. English disclosure information submitted to the KIND system of KRX is made available via its English language website dedicated to disclosure. Under an agreement between FSS and KRX, the disclosure information submitted to one platform is shared with the other.[7]

A notable exemption from these disclosure requirements applies to listed companies that feature less than 5% of shareholding by foreign investors. At the same time, policymakers and KRX support the new obligations with knowledge support or financial incentives, such as the offering of training in English disclosure practices or a reduction or waiver of listing fees.

### 1.    Public Offers

Only publicly offered bonds are able to be listed on KRX, though a listing remains optional. Specific conditions for disclosure of KRX-listed bonds, including SRI bonds, are shown in the next two subsections.

### 3.    Debt Securities Listed on Korea Exchange

Bonds listed on the KRX market are subject to the recently introduced English disclosure requirement if the issuer also has their stock listed on KRX (i.e., on the KOSPI [main] market segment). At the same time, issuers who only list their publicly offered bonds on KRX do not fall under the new English disclosure requirement.

The English disclosure requirement applies to corporate information on the issuer, not the details of a bond, with a particular focus on material changes, management decisions, and the financial statements, as well as any material related to the suspension or resumption of the trading of the issuer's stock. Disclosure obligations, including mandatory English disclosure obligations where they apply, follow the prescriptions in the KRX disclosure rules, specifically Paragraph 48 (Disclosure in English Language) and Paragraph 118-4 of the Detailed Rules of the KOSPI Market Disclosure Regulation (English Disclosure).[8]

Additional information on these and other KRX rules can be found in section J in this chapter. Disclosure requirements specific to SRI bonds are explained in the next subsection.

### 4.    Socially Responsible Investment Bonds Listed on Korea Exchange [New]

Bonds issued under the purview of the K-Taxonomy and relevant industry guidelines are referred to as SRI bonds when listed on KRX but may also be called ESG, thematic, or social contribution bonds in the market (see Chapter III.B for details).

The issuers of these SRI bonds listed on KRX and registered on the dedicated SRI segment provided by KRX (see Chapter III.H for details) are subject to additional disclosure obligations under the KRX disclosure rules due to the nature of SRI bonds. The additional information is also available on the dedicated SRO bond web page of KRX.

---

[7] FSS provides access to corporate filings for foreign investors via the English language version of its Data Analysis, Retrieval, and Transfer System, which can be accessed at https://englishdart.fss.or.kr/about/engAbout1.do#:~:text=DART%20(Data%20Analysis%2C%20Retrieval%20and ,to%20investors%20and%20other%20users. The KRX English language disclosure website, also known as the KIND system, may be found here at https://engkind.krx.co.kr/main.do?method=loadInitPage&scrnmode=1.

[8] The official title of the disclosure rules issued by KRX is the KOSPI Market Disclosure Regulation; the term "regulation" is adopted since the rules have to be approved by the FSC and are quasi-legal as a result.

Issuers must identify the nature of the bond (e.g., green or social bond) and cite the principles and guidelines under which the SRI bond was issued. Additional documents for registration in the SRI segment include

(i)   the sustainable bond management framework,
(ii)  external evaluation documents,
(iii) post-issuance reporting documents, and
(iv)  other reference materials as requested by KRX.

Changes to the sustainable bond management framework or provisions for the use of proceeds or other specific bond conditions then form part of the continuous disclosure obligations of the SRI bond issuer.

## H.    Self-Regulatory Organizations in the Korean Bond Market

KOFIA, KRX, and KSD remain the three designated SROs in the Korean bond market; however, the introduction of the Electronic Securities Act in 2019 had an impact on their function and/or ability to carry out rulemaking, as explained below.

### 1.    Korea Financial Investment Association

KOFIA operates the OTC marketplace and provides bond quotations and pricing information via its K-Bond platform. KOFIA manages its members on the basis of a membership agreement through which KOFIA can limit or suspend the activities of members who are deemed to have violated provisions in the membership agreement and corresponding OTC regulations set by KOFIA. At the same time, KOFIA does not have the power to supervise and regulate the OTC market or its participants directly, according to the stipulations and provisions of the FSCMA. If violations of FSCMA provisions occur, KOFIA will refer such violations to the FSS.

KOFIA offers three different types of membership: regular, associate, and special. Regular members consist of authorized financial investment business entities and some registered financial investment business entities. Associate members consist of some registered financial investment business entities and concurrently run financial investment entities. Special members include financial-investment-related institutions, general administrative service companies, fund and bond pricing companies, and credit rating agencies. As of December 2023, KOFIA had 400 regular members, 140 associate members, and 28 special members.

In addition to its previous remit, KOFIA was designated in June 2023 as the administrator that calculates the certificate of deposit interest rate (CD rate), a critical benchmark rate; the CD rate calculated by KOFIA took effect as a critical benchmark rate in accordance with the Act on the Management of Financial Benchmarks on 2 October 2023. Details on the critical benchmark rates and related developments can be found in Chapter IV.K.

### 2.    Korea Securities Depository

KSD handles the settlement of securities traded on KRX as well as the settlement of equities and bonds traded in the OTC market, currently processing a daily settlement volume of KRW25 trillion. At the end of 2023, KSD held electronic and deposited securities valued at KRW6,622 trillion, while KSD participants totaled 1,350—comprising financial institutions, including securities companies, banks, and insurance companies.

As an SRO, KSD sets rules for its operation and participants. Changes to KSD rules require approval from the FSC. Since the establishment of the Electronic Securities Act, 2019, changes to the Regulation of Electronic Registration Services for Stocks, Bonds, etc. require the prior approval of the MOJ, in addition to the FSC.

From 18 April 2022, KSD also assumed the role of calculating agent for the Korea Overnight Financing Repo Rate (KOFR), a critical benchmark rate pursuant to the Act on the Management of Financial Benchmarks. Details on the critical benchmark rates can be found in Chapter X.A.4.

## I.    Rules Related to Licensing and Trading Conventions

After the introduction of the Electronic Securities Act, 2019, participants must be an account management institution under the Regulation of Electronic Registration Service for Stocks, Bonds, etc.; meet the requirements as set forth in this regulation as well as in the Detailed Rules of KSD; and have sufficient human resources, computer systems, and other tangible facilities to perform the work as a settlement member.

## J.    Rules Related to Bond Listing or Registration, Trading, and Disclosure

### 1.    Over-the-Counter Market Rules Issued by the Korea Financial Investment Association

There have been no significant changes to KOFIA rules pertaining to the OTC bond market in recent years.

In January 2023, KOFIA issued Guidelines on ESG Bonds Ratings, with the intention to help credit rating agencies (who are members of KOFIA) assess relevant bonds and notes; the guidelines are considered a code of conduct and describe essential procedures for the evaluation of ESG bonds.

At the same time, KOFIA does not prescribe specific disclosure requirements for ESG bonds in the OTC market segment.

### 2.    Rules of Korea Exchange

Key among the KRX rule revisions was the need to include changes to disclosure obligations in the English language (see section G for details) for issuers listed on the KOSPI market. Consequently, KRX amended its KOSPI Market Disclosure Regulation effective 29 March 2023.[9]

KRX released the Guidelines for Operation of Segment Dedicated to SRI Bonds in December 2019. The guidelines (i) apply to bonds to be listed on KRX markets and registered in the SRI Bonds segment; (ii) explain the SRI Bonds website and the need for use of proceeds for projects that are eco-friendly or generate social benefits; and (iii) describe what companies that want to issue green, social, sustainability, and sustainability-linked

---

[9] The KOSPI Market Disclosure Regulation is available for download in English from the KRX website at https://sribond.krx.co.kr/en/05/05040000/SRI05040000.jsp. The term "regulation" is adopted to reflect the need for the FSC to approve KRX rules and their changes, thereby giving such regulations a quasi-legal character.

bonds in the Korean market need to do. The guidelines were followed by the establishment of the actual SRI Bonds website by KRX in June 2020.[10]

Until then, there had been no institution with public confidence that provided official information and statistics on SRI bonds; hence, it had been difficult for investors, especially foreign investors, to get relevant information in one location, as each SRI bond issuer disclosed SRI bond information separately. As an SRO and a market institution dedicated to disclosure, KRX provided confident and transparent information on SRI bonds with the publication of the guidelines and, subsequently, the SRI Bonds website.

More information on SRI bonds can be found in Chapter III.B, while the SRI Bonds website is covered in more detail in Chapter IV.F.[11]

## K.    Market Entry Requirements (Nonresidents)

Given that interest in the Korean bond market is likely to rise significantly following the implementation of policy measures designed to improve the market, particularly for nonresident investors (see relevant sections throughout this update note), this section provides a detailed overview of the revised or prevailing requirements and obligations for nonresident issuers and investors for easy reference. Details provided are as of March 2024.

### 1.    Nonresident Issuers

Nonresident issuers can issue bonds or notes in the Korean bond market. Some specific reporting requirements or conditions will apply when issuing bonds or notes in the Korean bond market, regardless of whether in Korean won or a foreign currency. All listings are subject to KRX listing and market rules (referred to as "KRX regulations") in their respective latest version (see also the previous section).

A foreign company is required to file a report on such issuance of bonds or notes with the MOEF, with the report to be submitted prior to carrying out any foreign exchange or remittance of the bond or note proceeds, under provisions in the Foreign Exchange Transactions Act: Article 15 (1) and Article 18 (1)(2).

### 2.    Foreign Investors

For many years, market participants and observers had perceived the Korean market as difficult to enter and to operate in. Documentation and approval requirements, operating hours, limited use of English, restrictions on transaction types, and resulting higher costs were frequently mentioned as key hurdles. The Government of the Republic of Korea recognized the importance of providing a more open and investor-friendly capital market and put forward a set of policy measures, beginning in 2023, to remove real or perceived barriers. Key among these policy measures have been the abolition of the IRC, market access via ICSDs, and the ability to access and transact in the foreign exchange market more freely. These changes are detailed below, while information on the legal and regulatory basis is described in the next section.

---

[10] KRX is currently considering changing the term "SRI bonds" to "ESG bonds" in the near future; KOFIA is already referring to such bonds as ESG bonds.

[11] The guidelines, as well as other KRX rules and underlying regulations, are available from the SRI Bonds website of KRX at https://sribond.krx.co.kr/en/05/05040000/SRI05040000.jsp.

a.    Direct Market Access—Introduction of Legal Entity Identifier
      for Foreign Investors

With the abolition of the IRC concept in December 2023 (see section M.1 in this
chapter), new foreign (nonresident) investors are now able to access the Korean
capital market by simply providing an LEI and supporting constituent documents or
passport information in the case of individual investors, as is typically required for the
opening of a new account. An approval from a regulatory body is no longer required,
and interactions are limited to those between the investor and any market
intermediaries the investor appoints.

The LEI now represents the investor identification in all market activities for a new
foreign investor and is also used to identify the investor in regulatory reporting by
market parties.

According to guidance from the FSC, existing IRC holders will need to continue using
their IRC in all market transactions and will continue to be able to amend their IRC,
amounting to a reissuance of the IRC (e.g., in the case of changes at the investor).
Existing IRC holders will not be able to replace their IRC with an LEI (or passport
details in the case of an individual investor) and will be restricted from opening a new
account with an LEI or passport number under the regulation. If a foreign investor
with an existing IRC opens a new account with their LEI, it will be considered a
violation of related regulations and may result in disadvantages in exercising rights.[12]

For institutional investors new to the Korean market, custodians (as a standing proxy)
and every securities firm through which an investor intends to trade will need the LEI
and documents that support the authenticity of the LEI, as well as the investing
entity's constituting documents for their real name verification, just as would be the
case in any know-your-customer (KYC) or account-opening process. A guidance
jointly provided by KOFIA, Koscom, KRX, and KSD to market participants states that
the status of the LEI should be "fully corroborated" to proceed with account opening,
meaning that sufficient information is found in authoritative public records to
corroborate all data supplied by the applicant.

According to the guidance, documents for validation of a foreign investor's real name
include, but may not be limited to, the following:

- documents related to corporate registration included in the original LEI
  application (as requested by the entity issuing the LEI, or the Local Operating
  Unit); and
- a certificate of residence or certificate of good standing, in the form of a letter,
  confirmation, or certificate issued by the government or designated in the
  economy of residence of the investor.[13]

Individual market intermediaries may have additional documentation requirements.
Documents will need to be presented in physical form; while market participants are
looking into the use of electronic submission of documents with digital signatures, at
the time of publication of this update note, such practice was not yet supported.

---

[12] Restrictions relate, for example, to the acquisition of listed stock with ownership limits and monitoring for
supervision purposes.
[13] Information and reference are provided here with the kind permission of KRX, KOFIA, KSD, and Koscom.
At present, the note is only available in Korean, as it is intended for domestic market participants only. Koscom is a
financial information technology firm founded by the then Ministry of Finance and KRX; it is owned by KRX.

The documents should be in English or, if issued in another language, be accompanied by a translation into English. Under established market practice, supporting (corporate) documents may need to be notarized in their economy of origin; certified-true copies are generally not accepted. The real-name-verification process follows the Guideline for Real-Name Financial Transactions established by the Korea Federation of Banks and reviewed by the FSC. The guideline mandates notarization solely for the power of attorney when application documents of a foreign entity are submitted through an agent. A list of potential alternatives to a certificate of residence (as prescribed by the National Tax Service [NTS]) that are accepted in the context of taxation but may also be accepted in the Korean market at large can be found in Table 6.5 of Chapter VI.H.

Since the abolition of the IRC concept, the investor registration relies on these real-name-verification and KYC processes (previously, the IRC form and documents were processed by the custodian as standing proxy and a copy of the actual IRC certificate itself was then shared with other market participants). However, as part of the new practice, custodians (who often are the first point of contact) would accept the foreign investor's LEI and supporting documents, obtain or compile a KYC form (containing all necessary information), and typically share the form (and/or supporting documents) with the securities firms where the new client wants to open accounts. While it is the foreign investor's obligation to furnish every financial institution with the documents necessary for identification, the foreign investor can formally instruct its custodian to circulate the information the investor submitted to the custodian about identification to other financial institutions with which the investor plans to open accounts or through whom the investor intends to transact.

In this regard, it should be noted that the IRC was assigned once and had no expiry date. In contrast, LEI have a validity of 1 year and need to be renewed on an annual basis. There is no regulatory requirement in the Korean market to ensure the ongoing validity of the LEI once the account has been opened, though intermediaries may be subject to additional regulatory requirements in their home market. Investors bear the risk associated with an invalid LEI and need to notify market intermediaries if the status of their LEI changes.

### b.    Indirect Market Access via International Central Securities Depositories

While many of the recent policy changes and announcements are relevant for investors in all asset classes in the Korean capital market, this particular policy measure only applies to the bond market, in fact only to investments in KTBs and MSBs. As such, only bond investors may avail themselves of this indirect market access route via the ICSDs.

As part of recent policy measures to improve the attractiveness of the Korean capital market, foreign investors will be offered the option to transact Korean government bonds through their accounts in ICSDs. The concept is typically referred to in the Korean market as the "revitalization of the omnibus account," since the omnibus account concept has existed in principle for a number of years (see section M for context).

According to the MOEF, when the omnibus account is reactivated, foreign investors will be able to invest through their ICSD accounts that they already have regardless of the existing procedures such as appointing the standing proxy (typically a custodian) and opening a domestic trading account. The Government Bond Policy Division of the MOEF intends to officially release reference material for the new market entry option at the end of April 2024, with a more detailed explanation of the ICSD omnibus account.[14]

Consequently, the market entry process described under subsection a. above would not apply. Instead, eligible ICSDs will open and maintain omnibus accounts directly with KSD as the central securities depository and electronic register (see also Chapter II.C), while opening and maintaining omnibus cash accounts with an appointed domestic settlement bank. At the same time—since the Korean won may not be transacted or held outside of the Republic of Korea—investors would have to appoint a correspondent bank in the Republic of Korea to execute FX transactions to fund Korean won for settlement, under the third-party FX option recently introduced through the revision of the MOEF Regulation on Foreign Exchange Transaction (see also section M.7 in this chapter). In a recent announcement, the MOEF also offered investors the opportunity to use their existing Korean won accounts to transfer funds to the ICSD omnibus cash account for the settlement of transactions.[15]

From their perspective, foreign investors may transact Korean government bonds through their established trading platforms and instruct settlement via their appointed ICSD. Additionally, the investor would arrange a domestic FX trade, as necessary, with its appointed FX bank. The ICSD would in turn settle all such client transactions with domestic settlement counterparties in KSD and effect payments through its cash correspondent upon receipt of funding from the clients' domestic cash correspondents. Instruction formats and market-specific indicators or practices to be observed by clients would follow the prescriptions of each ICSD and may be subject to limitations that affect certain client types and instruments.

Clearstream S.A. and Euroclear Bank have so far been named as the ICSDs becoming members of KSD.[16] For more information about this access route, eligibility, and applicable practices, interested parties are advised to contact their ICSD.

## M.    Regulations and Limitations Relevant for Nonresidents

The information in this section focuses on details of the relevant changes to requirements and obligations affecting nonresident investors under recently introduced policy measures. The new concessions offered to nonresidents are added to the original list of topics in the *ASEAN+3 Bond Market Guide Republic of Korea*. Details provided are as of March 2024.

The replacement process following the IRC abolition is explained in detail in the previous section, as is the additional indirect market access option for foreign investors via ICSDs. New measures include a raft of changes in relation to the foreign exchange market in the Republic of Korea.

### 1.    Foreign Investor Registration

The need for nonresident investors to obtain an IRC to access the Korean capital market was abolished with effect from 14 December 2023. The IRC concept had been in use since 1992 and has often been cited as a hurdle in terms of ease of market access. The change

---

[14] Adapted from statements on p. 123 of MOEF. 2023. *Korea Treasury Bonds 2022*. Seoul. English versions of this and other annual KTB reports are available at https://ktb.moef.go.kr/eng/publications.do.

[15] See MOEF. 2024. International Investors' KRW Trading for Local Stocks and Bonds Investment To Be Easier. Press Release. 21 February. https://english.moef.go.kr/pc/selectTbPressCenterDtl.do?boardCd=N0001&seq=5783.

[16] To avoid ambiguity, it should be mentioned that, prior to the introduction of the Electronic Securities Act, 2019, participants in KSD were referred to as "depository members"; following the introduction of the act, "members" is considered more appropriate (as KSD's main role is as an electronic registry under the act).

demonstrated the willingness of policymakers to listen to market participant feedback and represents a key part of a broader set of policy measures to make the Korean capital market—including the bond market—more accessible and attractive to foreign investors.

The legal basis for the change was introduced in the revision bill of the Enforcement Decree of the FSCMA, approved by the Government of the Republic of Korea at a cabinet meeting on 5 June 2023. Consequently, regulatory authorities revised the FSC Regulation on Financial Investment Business and the FSS Detailed Rules of the Regulation on Financial Investment Business to reflect the change in process. The decree and regulations all took effect on 14 December 2023.

Following the abolition of the IRC concept, market registration for foreign investors in the form of a legal entity is achieved by providing an LEI and supporting documents (passport information for foreign individual investors) as part of the account opening process, a process that brings the Korean market in line with other regional and international markets. The LEI will be used as investor identification in market activities and needs to be provided to all domestic market entities that a foreign investor transacts investment business with in the Republic of Korea, including the custodian(s), other banks (e.g., for FX services), and securities firms. The LEI will also be used to identify a nonresident investor in statutory reporting to regulatory authorities.

Investors who had obtained an IRC in the past are required to continue to use the IRC in their transactional dealings to minimize any potential inconvenience otherwise caused by the change; investors may even amend their IRC—in case of, for example, name changes—or cancel a previously issued IRC if an investor withdraws from the Korean market.

Following the IRC's abolition, regulatory authorities will monitor total and individual foreign holding limits (on Korean equities and other instruments subject to limits) through a combination of IRC and LEI identifiers. The FSS is using the Foreign Investment Management System for that purpose.

6.    Access to the Korean Market via International Central Securities Depositories (Indirect Market Access) [New]

To increase interest in Korean government bonds from foreign investors and in preparation for the anticipated inclusion of these bonds in international bond indices (see also Chapter X.B), policymakers decided to reactivate the concept of allowing ICSDs to open a direct account at KSD to route the transactions of its foreign investor clients to the Korean market. This as an alternative to each foreign investor opening and maintaining their own cash and securities accounts with Korean intermediaries. A description of the current access option can be found in section K in this chapter, while this section focuses on providing some context for this policy measure.

The policy measure in fact is referenced in the Korean market as a "revitalization of the omnibus account" since the FSC Regulation on Financial Investment Business in principle allows the use of an omnibus account as a policy option (**Table 2.4**). While an earlier trial in 2017 promoted by the FSC and focusing on equities did not result in the actual opening of omnibus accounts—due to onerous and specific reporting requirements for each IRC using such option at the time—the MOEF has chosen to commence the rollout of this option as part of its overall policy measures to make the Korean capital market more attractive for foreign investors. The revitalization of the omnibus account through ICSDs has also been facilitated by the MOEF's decision to exempt foreign investors from withholding tax on interest and capital gains derived from government bonds (see Chapter VI.H for details).

Table 2.4: Comparison of Omnibus Account Types

| Omnibus Account Type | Omnibus Account for Stock Trading | Omnibus Account for Bond Trading (Indirect Market Access) |
|---|---|---|
| Government body in charge | FSC | MOEF |
| Introduction | 2017 | 2010 |
| Improvement or revitalization | 2023 (improvement) | 2024 (revitalization) |
| Statutory grounds | Subsidiary legislation of FSCMA | Subsidiary legislation of FSCMA |
| Major points | Streamlining relevant reporting processes in the Korean stock market | Providing alternative indirect access to the Korean bond market |

FSC = Financial Services Commission, FSCMA = Financial Services and Capital Market Act, MOEF = Ministry of Economy and Finance of Korea.
Source: ASEAN+3 Bond Market Forum compilation based on information adapted from FSC and MOEF press releases.

Yet, the asset types that can be transacted through the ICSD omnibus account are limited to KTBs and MSBs. While this restricts the use of this indirect market entry option to bond investors, the measure may offer future benefits for investors, such as the ability to use Korean government bonds in their ICSD accounts as collateral for other transactions.

The FSCMA and its subsidiary legislation did not originally contain any provisions on which type of entities may avail themselves of an omnibus account in principle. To establish a clear legal basis for the ICSD omnibus account, the Government of the Republic of Korea revised the FSC Regulation on Financial Investment Business on 13 June 2023 (with an effective date of 14 December 2023), while the remit of both the FSC and the FSS allows the determination of specific criteria for eligibility for this policy option. Consequently, the FSC also revised its Regulation on Financial Investment Business to stipulate (in Article 6-7) that Korean government bonds may be traded offshore between investors who maintain accounts with an intermediary organization (i.e., an ICSD) and settled in the domestic market using an omnibus account to be maintained directly with KSD. In its revision of the Detailed Rules of Regulation on Financial Investment Business (Article 5-1), the FSS subsequently clarified that the term "international depository and clearing organization" meant Clearstream and Euroclear. In consequence, presently only Clearstream S.A. and Euroclear Bank are able to open, maintain, and operate an omnibus account for Korean government bond transactions in the Korean market.

As of the end of 2023, KSD had signed an agent agreement with Clearstream and a CSD agreement with Euroclear to establish and operate omnibus account services for KTBs and MSBs, and it was in the process of implementing the necessary ICSD omnibus account system functionality, which was expected to go live in the first half of 2024. Instead of establishing a direct connection with KSD, both ICSDs will utilize SWIFT messaging to interact with KSD.

At the same time, the ICSD omnibus account option does come with a requirement for the ICSDs to furnish periodical and ad hoc reporting on the transactions conducted through the omnibus account, such as a record of transactions of the investors on a monthly basis. In the transaction details, to be submitted from the ICSD to the FSS via KSD, the full entity names of the foreign investors are to be included as well as the relevant LEI information for new foreign investors entering the market after 14 December 2023 (following the IRC's abolition).

The reporting obligation is stipulated in Article 5-1 (Paragraphs 2 and 3) of the FSS Detailed Rules of the Regulation on Financial Investment Business.

### 7.    Ability to Transact Foreign Exchange via Third Parties [New]

As part of its set of measures to make the Korean capital market more attractive for foreign investors, the MOEF set out the FX Market Structural Improvement Plan in February 2023. In its announcement, the MOEF clarified that nonresidents are able to execute FX transactions of Korean won against other currencies through any banks or authorized FX agents other than their appointed custodian bank; this practice is generally referred to as "third-party FX." The MOEF stated that this change in policy did not require changes to the Foreign Exchange Transaction Act, or FETA, and that it would issue a corresponding interpretive ruling to provide clarity to the market.[17] Consequently, the MOEF revised the MOEF Regulation on Foreign Exchange Transaction, effective 4 July 2023.

Previously, it was established market practice that nonresidents were able to execute transactions in the FX market only through dedicated accounts with their appointed custodian bank. While this was occasionally challenged by investors' understanding of the legal and regulatory framework, the practical aspect of funding through a third party, combined with penalties for failed settlements and statutory reporting requirements on all FX transactions and account movements by the custodian or any third party, discouraged the use of third-party FX.

The MOEF interpretive ruling will, at least in principle, allow nonresident investors to pursue best execution practices in the Korean FX market. At the same time, some of the procedural requirements may continue to make this greater flexibility impractical.

### 8.    Participation in the Domestic Foreign Exchange Market [New]

An additional measure announced in February 2023 as part of the MOEF's FX Market Structural Improvement Plan will be the ability for nonresident financial institutions to directly participate in the domestic FX market in the Republic of Korea.

Previously, the Korean domestic FX market was limited to domestic banks and non-bank financial institutions licensed as FX businesses. Nonresident investors or nonresidents in general were only able to conduct FX transactions through domestic market participants.

The new concession will require the registration of interested parties as a so-called Registered Foreign Institution (RFI). Upon successful registration, the RFI would be able to transact FX spots and forwards (FX swaps and outright forwards) with any counterparty in the domestic FX market directly. At the same time, RFIs will need to settle KRW transactions through a designated KRW account with a domestic bank.

The MOEF announced that the foreign exchange market reform measures will be officially implemented from the second half of 2024 after 6 months of pilot operation. The MOEF established the Guidelines on the Foreign Exchange Affairs of Foreign Financial institutions and enforced them from 7 November 2023.

---

[17] The MOEF has set up a dedicated web page, "FX Market Reform," that offers press releases, guidelines for market participants, relevant laws and regulations, updates on developments, and a list of practical frequently asked questions. The web page is available in English and Korean at https://www.moef.go.kr/sns/2024/foreignExchange.do?category=lawEng.

# III

# Characteristics of the Korean Bond Market

Global developments, such as the move toward sustainable finance, and a number of policy measures implemented or announced by the Government of the Republic of Korea have changed the Korean bond market significantly—and will continue to do so—since the publication of the *ASEAN+3 Bond Market Guide Republic of Korea* in May 2018.

These changes or additions to the Korean bond market's characteristics are described in this chapter in the context of the existing structure of the *ASEAN+3 Bond Market Guide Republic of Korea*. New features are added at the end of each original section and are indicated accordingly.

## A.    Definition of Securities

The rapid growth of sustainable finance instruments in the Korean market—referred to as SRI bonds, ESG bonds, or social contribution bonds—and the government's announcement to establish a framework for digital assets offer the opportunity to expand this section within the original structure of the bond market guide. It is anticipated that existing laws and regulations will continue to be amended and new laws formulated to define new debt securities and asset types that have characteristics of traditional debt securities but exist only in electronic or digital form, while also adding new features.

### 1.    Conventional Debt Securities

The definition for conventional debt securities can be found in Article 4 (3) of the FSCMA:

> The term "debt securities" in this Act means state (government) bonds, local government bonds, special bonds (referring to bonds issued by a corporation established by direct operation of an Act; hereinafter the same shall apply), corporate bonds, corporate commercial papers (referring to promissory notes issued by a company for raising the funds required for its business, which shall meet the requirements prescribed by Presidential Decree; hereinafter the same shall apply), and other similar instruments, which bear the indication of a right to claim the payment.

### 2.    Sustainable Finance Instruments

The range of bond types available in the Korean market has expanded considerably in recent years, particularly in line with the global development toward sustainable finance. The Korean market now also features a variety of sustainable finance instruments in the bond market, with substantial issuance in both the domestic and international markets, and in local and foreign currencies. The instrument types typically issued in the domestic bond market are further detailed here.

Green or sustainable finance instruments in the Korean bond market are alternatively referred to as SRI, ESG, thematic, or social contribution bonds. The use of terms may depend on the market institution or on market segment practice.

The key drivers of the new securities types were the establishment of the K-Taxonomy and the simultaneous publication of the K-Taxonomy Guidelines by the MOE in December 2021. The K-Taxonomy defined which economic activities were considered green or sustainable, while the K-Taxonomy Guidelines provided implementation guidance, particularly to avoid greenwashing and to address capital flows into green activities.[18]

In December 2020, the MOE and the FSC, with consultation from KRX and the Korea Environmental Industry & Technology Institute, published the Korean Green Bond Guideline, which are often referenced as "K-GBG" in the market, to fill the void of official market guidance and provide market participants with a clearer standard on what are true green economic activities. Establishing how green bonds are defined was necessary given the growth in issuance of green bonds in the Korean market since 2018.[19]

According to the K-GBG, green bonds are

> Bonds (i) the proceeds of which are used for "green projects" that meet six environmental objectives and (ii) which satisfy the four core components of the Green Bond Principles formulated by the International Capital Market Association, which consist of (a) use of proceeds, (b) process for project evaluation and selection, (c) management of proceeds, and (d) reporting.

In response to the initial green bond issuances in 2018, KRX published the Guidelines for Operation of Segment Dedicated to SRI Bonds (SRI Guidelines) in December 2019 to help define which instruments may be considered SRI bonds and which requirements are imposed on potential issuers to be able to list on the SBI bonds segment of KRX, such as eco-friendliness, use of proceeds, and generation of social benefits. For more information on the SRI Bonds website operated by KRX, please see Chapter IV.F.4.[20]

Brief descriptions of ESG and SRI bond types are provided in later subsections.

### 3.    Digital or Virtual Assets

The Government of the Republic of Korea announced the formulation of a comprehensive legal and regulatory framework for digital assets in August 2022, with the aim of establishing a Digital Asset Basic Act as fundamental legislation, while amending existing laws and regulations to accommodate necessary definitions and characteristics of digital assets.

The Electronic Securities Act, 2019, which intended to enshrine the concept of dematerialization in the securities market, is considered a step in this direction and is expected to be further amended to this end.

---

[18] The K-Taxonomy and the K-Taxonomy Guidelines are available in English from the website of the MOE at https://www.me.go.kr/skin/doc.html?fn=20230831172157.pdf&rs=/upload_private/preview/.

[19] Information in this section based on MOE press releases as well as legal commentary in the public domain and media reports on the K-Taxonomy and related publications. The K-GBG is variously referenced as the Korean Green Bond Guideline, Korean Green Bond Guidelines, or green bond issuance guidelines in official announcements and media reports.

[20] The SRI Guidelines are available for download in English from the KRX website at https://sribond.krx.co.kr/en/05/05040000/SRI05040000.jsp.

In Article 2 (Definitions), the Act on the Protection of Virtual Asset Users contains a definition of virtual assets:

> The term "virtual asset"" means electronic certificates (including all associated rights) that have economic value and that can be traded or transferred electronically [...]

It also lists a number of exclusions that are not considered virtual assets, including

(i)   tangible and intangible products obtained through the use of game products,
(ii)  electronic prepayment means,
(iii) electronically registered stocks,
(iv)  electronic bills, and
(v)   digital currencies issued by the BOK.

The act also defines virtual asset service providers, including intermediaries, and is expected to become effective on 19 July 2024.

## B.    Types of Bonds and Notes

This section contains a brief summary of major instrument types, focusing on those instruments that have been recently introduced in the bond market. Individual features of these bonds are further explained in the next section. For ease of reference, the enumeration of sections follows the original *ASEAN+3 Bond Market Guide Republic of Korea*.

### 1.    Bonds and Notes Categorized by Type of Issuer

#### a.    Government Bonds

Korean government bonds, known as KTBs, continue to be issued with tenors of 3, 5, 10, 20, 30, and 50 years—with the government increasingly focused on a lengthening of maturities in response to market demand. All tenors represent fixed-interest bonds, while the 10-year KTB is also issued as an inflation-linked product that is referred to as a KTBi. Coupon rates of KTBs are set to multiples of 0.125% and interest is paid semi-annually.[21]

In addition, the Government of the Republic of Korea issues National Housing Bonds and Foreign Exchange Stabilization Fund Bonds.

The government also started issuing green and sustainability bonds in 2019 under the Foreign Exchange Equalization Fund Bond program.

#### c.    Special (Purpose) Bonds

This type of bond comprises issuances by the BOK, government-owned and special purpose institutions, or other statutory entities in the Republic of Korea. More recently, these institutions have been driving public sector issuance of green, social, and other sustainable finance instruments.

---

[21] General information such as the issuance calendar as well as issuance segmentation statistics can be found on the MOEF website at https://ktb.moef.go.kr/eng/abtKtbs.do.

In fact, the Korea Development Bank issued the first green bond and the first social bond in the Korean domestic bond market, both in 2018. The same year, the first sustainability bond was issued by the Export–Import Bank of Korea in the domestic market; this institution had tapped the international bond market for green bonds as early as 2013. In terms of their characteristics, these bonds did not substantially differ from other sustainable finance instruments issued in the Republic of Korea (see also new section 8).

Falling into this category of regularly issued instruments are the MSBs issued by the BOK as part of its open market operation. In contrast to most money market instruments, MSBs typically have maturities longer than 1 year and up to 3 years, hence the designation as bonds. MSBs are issued at a discount and repaid at par. MSB issuance and bidding processes are subject to the BOK's Open Market Operations Regulations as well as related rules.[22]

### d.    Private Sector Bonds (Corporate Bonds)

In addition to conventional bonds, corporate issuers have been issuing green bonds or other thematic finance instruments in the Korean market since 2019 (see section 9).

### 8.    Socially Responsible Investment Bonds (ESG or Thematic Bonds) [New]

This new categorization—in the Korean market also referred to as ESG, thematic, or social contribution bonds—was established following the issuance of green, social, and sustainability bonds by Korean institutions in the domestic market in 2018. These SRI bond categories also include sustainability-linked bonds as well as transition bonds.

The following year, the MOE published its K-Taxonomy, describing for the first time what would constitute green or sustainable economic activities in the context of the Korean economy. The K-Taxonomy was followed by the K-Taxonomy Guidelines, aimed at translating the designated sustainable economic activities into actionable activities in Korean financial markets.

Among the green financing mechanisms described in the K-Taxonomy Guidelines, green bond issuance is the most common way used by corporations and financial institutions in the Republic of Korea. To meet the prescriptions in the guidelines for green economic activities, potential issuers need to meet the K-Taxonomy requirements in categories such as activity, accreditation, exclusion, and protection. To offer further guidance to potential issuers and other market participants, the MOE and the FSC jointly issued the K-GBG, which were last revised in December 2022.

The following subsections offer basic definitions for SRI, or thematic, bonds; the definitions are adapted from the SRI Guideline issued by KRX.[23] While the basic characteristics of SRI bonds are the same as conventional bonds, the main difference—other than the declaration of use of proceeds and other relevant features under the aspired thematic bond category—typically lies in the certification process required to designate a bond an SRI bond. Similar to other markets, issuers must establish a green or sustainable bond framework (see also section H) to signal their intentions and readiness to the market, and declare how they will pursue green or sustainable economic activities. An external reviewer then certifies that the framework complies with established international standards and/or with the K-Taxonomy or K-GBG. Details of these requirements are provided under sections H and I in this chapter.

---

[22] Details on MSB issuance and auction processes, issuance notices, and the underlying rules can be found on the following BOK website at https://www.bok.or.kr/eng/main/contents.do?menuNo=400402.

[23] For details, see https://sribond.krx.co.kr/en/05/05040000/SRI05040000.jsp.

In the Republic of Korea, bond frameworks do not have to follow the K-Taxonomy but instead are most often aligned to the Green Bond Principles or other thematic principles maintained by the International Capital Market Association (ICMA). At the same time, however, the K-Taxonomy is largely aligned with such international standards.[24]

### a.    Green Bonds

Green bonds are issued to raise funds for environmentally friendly projects and other social infrastructure.

### b.    Social Bonds

Social bonds are issued to raise funds for social value creation projects. In fact, social bonds represent the largest category of SRI, or thematic, bonds in the domestic Korean bond market.

### c.    Sustainability Bonds

Sustainability bonds are issued to raise funds for environmentally friendly and social value creation projects.

### d.    Sustainability-Linked Bonds

Sustainability-linked bonds are instruments in which the financial or structural characteristics can change depending on whether the issuer achieves the predetermined sustainability goals.

### e.    Transition Bonds

The K-Taxonomy includes definitions of the transition sector as well as transition activities. However, at the time of publication of this update note, a dedicated guideline for transition bonds had not been established and no transition bonds had been issued in the Republic of Korea's domestic bond market, nor had a transition bond classification been established on the SRI Bonds website of KRX.

SRI bonds in the Korean market are typically issued to the public and listed on KRX, which hosts a dedicated SRI bond segment (see also Chapter IV). The OTC bond market presently does not have a dedicated SRI or ESG bond section and, at the time of the publication of this update note, did not specifically track SRI or ESG bonds in the market.

As of the end of 2023, the MOE was conducting a pilot program to offer subsidies for the interest costs of green bonds. A group of 23 public and private companies were participating in the program for the subsidization of the difference in the interest for green bond issuance. They planned to issue green bonds worth around KRW3.9 trillion by the end of that year, at an estimated cost of approximately KRW5.1 billion.

Successful implementation of the projects supported by these bonds was expected to lead to significant environmental improvements, including a reduction of approximately 3.73 million tons of greenhouse gas emissions annually.

---

[24] Details on the Green Bond Principles, Social Bond Principles, Sustainability Bond Guidelines, and Sustainability-Linked Bond Principles can be found on the ICMA website at https://www.icmagroup.org/sustainable-finance/.

## E.    Methods of Issuing Bonds and Notes (Primary Market)

While there have been no substantial changes in the issuance methods and practices in the Korean bond market since the publication of the *ASEAN+3 Bond Market Guide Republic of Korea*, a number of small corrections, changes, and one addition to the auction process for government bonds are mentioned in this section.

### 2.    Issuance Methods by Issuer Type

This section contains a description of some corrections and changes to the auction process.

#### d.    Government Securities

##### ii.    Dutch or Single-Price Auction

Variously referred to as Dutch auction or single-price auction by the BOK and the MOEF, under this scheme all winning bidders pay the price of the lowest successful bid.

##### iii.    Differential Auction

A differential auction is a mixture of the two main methods. In this method, the accepted bid yield is determined by categorizing all bid yields into groups at intervals of 3–4 basis points in ascending order and by selecting the highest bid yield in each group (**Table 3.5**).

Table 3.5: Examples of Determining the Successful Bidding Yield by Auction Type

| Primary Dealer | Bidding Conditions | Cut-Off Yield by Auction Type | | |
| --- | --- | --- | --- | --- |
| | | Dutch | Conventional | Differential-Price (example: 5 bps) |
| A | 2.955%, KRW20 billion | All 3.055% | 2.955% | 2.995% |
| B | 3.000%, KRW20 billion | | 3.000% | 3.005% |
| C | 3.005%, KRW20 billion | | 3.005% | |
| D | 3.020%, KRW10 billion | | 3.020% | 3.055% |
| E | 3.055%, KRW10 billion | | 3.055% | |
| F | 3.070%, KRW20 billion | Failed bid | Failed bid | Failed bid |

bps = basis points, KRW = Korean won.
Note: A comparable table was included in the *ASEAN+3 Bond Market Guide Republic of Korea* as Figure 3.3.
Source: Adapted from p. 57 of Ministry of Economy and Finance. *Korea Treasury Bonds, 2022.*
https://english.moef.go.kr/pm/KoreaTreasuryBondList.do.

Using the example in the table, under a differential price auction, for example, the highest cut-off yield is 3.055% (of Primary Dealer E), the bid yields are divided into groups of "3.055~3.010," "3.005~2.960%," and "2.955~2.910%." Each group's highest bid yield—3.055%, 3.005%, and 2.955%, respectively—becomes the successful bidding group.

### iv.    Non-Competitive Bidding

Three non-competitive bid options have existed for KTB auctions and were described in the *ASEAN+3 Bond Market Guide Republic of Korea*.

With effect from 2021, the MOEF introduced a fourth non-competitive bid option that allows primary dealers to exercise such option based on the results of the competitive auction bids. The MOEF sets aside up to 20% of the total size of a KTB issuance for this and the other non-competitive bid options.

The intention for this so-called "non-competitive bid option IV" is to minimize the volatility that might arise from a large issuance and, at the same time, help the MOEF to achieve its issuance target. This bid option is conducted on the third Friday of the issuance month, with the actual target issuance amount announced on the second Thursday of the issuance month. The likely KTB types are shorter-tenored issuances, such as 2-year to 5-year issues, but the MOEF may also offer longer-tenored issues if it so deems necessary.[25]

## G.    Language of Documentation and Disclosure Items

The information provided here on the language of documentation and disclosure items in the Korean market supplements or adjusts previous statements in the same section in the *ASEAN+3 Bond Market Guide Republic of Korea*, particularly in recognition of the increase in interest in the use of the English language in ASEAN+3 professional bond markets.

Beginning in 2024, corporations whose stocks are listed on KRX—on its KOSPI main market—will be required to provide disclosure in the English language in addition to Korean; the issuer's asset size matters and a phased approach applies. This measure is part of the strategy by policymakers to improve the accessibility of the Korean market for nonresident investors. The accompanying FSC press release noted that, in 2022, only about 13.8% of Korean disclosure for listed companies had also been made available in English.[26]

This disclosure obligation applies to both equities and bonds (see section 4 below), in fact all issued securities from an issuer, if that issuer has its stock listed on KRX. If the issuer is stock-listed on KRX, this includes bonds that are registered in the OTC market (i.e., on the KOFIA platform). However, the disclosure relates to information about the company, not the bonds. The English language disclosure will need to be made within 3 days from when a disclosure was made in Korean. The disclosure obligations itself follow the listing requirements or other existing prescriptions in the markets, with a particular emphasis on financial statements, continuous disclosure of material events, and the suspension or resumption of trading.

For a more detailed description of these disclosure obligations and how they apply to different types of issuers, please see Chapter II.G.

---

[25] Text adopted from MOEF. 2023. *Korea Treasury Bonds, 2022.*
https://english.moef.go.kr/pm/KoreaTreasuryBondList.do.

[26] FSC. 2023. Item IV: Expand the Availability of English Disclosures in Phases. Press Release. 25 January.
https://www.fsc.go.kr/eng/pr010101/79346.

### 4.    Bonds Listed on Korea Exchange

Issuers that have listed bonds on KRX previously had the option to provide disclosure information on these bonds in English within 1 week of the disclosure in Korean. The introduction of the new English disclosure obligations in 2024 does not automatically change this—corporates who only have listed bonds on KRX are not affected by the new measure.

For issuers whose stock is listed on KRX, disclosure in English may no longer be optional, depending on the company size and other factors (see details above). If these companies also have bonds listed on KRX (e.g., the KOSPI or SRI Bonds segments), information on the issuer in bond disclosures is also to be made in English. Items to be disclosed in English follow the KRX listing and disclosure rules in their respective latest version. Particular emphasis is put on disclosures relating to material events in the management of the company, including the making of important decisions, and to financial statements and any suspension or resumption of trading of the company stock.[27]

KRX provides an English language disclosure information portal, with corporate disclosure items, market alerts, as well as information on new listings.[28]

### 5.    Bonds Issued and Traded in the Over-the-Counter Market [New]

This section has been added to clarify that bonds issued and traded in the OTC market are not subject to the new English disclosure obligations described above, unless the issuer also has its stock listed on the KOSPI market.

## H.    Registration of Debt Securities

In contrast to previous market practice, the term "registration" in the context of securities, and specifically debt securities, is now also used for debt securities listed on KRX, both for bonds that qualify as SRI bonds and also pursuant to the introduction of the electronic securities system under the Electronic Securities Act, 2019.

### 3.    Registration of Debt Securities at Korea Exchange [New]

Two forms of registrations are now associated with debt securities listed on KRX, in addition to the act of listing itself (see section I), as explained below. These registrations typically occur in parallel to the listing process.

#### a.    Registration for Socially Responsible Investment Bonds Segment

KRX requires a registration of debt securities that are eligible for and intended to be included in its dedicated SRI Bonds segment.

SRI bonds that meet the registration requirements as per the SRI guidelines issued by KRX are registered in the SRI Bonds segment upon application from the issuer. The registration requirements are as follows:

---

[27] KRX listing and disclosure rules may be found at
https://global.krx.co.kr/contents/GLB/06/0601/0601000000/GLB0601000000.jsp.
[28] For details, see https://engkind.krx.co.kr/main.do?method=loadInitPage&scrnmode=1#.

(i)  The bond must be listed or scheduled to be listed on the exchange's bond market and comply with the principles and guidelines.

(ii) A bond management framework needs to have been established.

(iii) An evaluation report from an external reviewer needs to be submitted, stating that the bond management framework complies with the relevant principles such as the ICMA Green Bond Principles, other relevant principles, or the K-GBG.

(iv) As additional documents, green, social, and sustainability bonds require the submission of use-of-proceeds documents, while sustainability-linked bonds require the submission of an investment prospectus.

The bond management framework for green, social, and sustainability bonds needs to detail four key elements: (i) the use of proceeds, (ii) the process for project evaluation and selection, (iii) the management of proceeds, and (iv) reporting. It typically also references the principles to which the sustainable character of the bond is aligned. In the case of sustainability-linked bonds, the framework needs to contain the following five key elements: (i) key performance indicators, (ii) sustainability performance targets set by the issuer, (iii) bond characteristics, (iv) reporting, and (v) verification.

Among the ongoing registration requirements—and not unlike the actual listing requirements—are the obligations for the issuer to provide regular post-issuance reporting through the submission of a (i) use-of-proceeds report and impact report for green, social, and sustainability bonds; or (ii) a performance report and external evaluation report for sustainability-linked bonds.

A revocation of a registration occurs upon redemption of the bond and may occur if the issuer applies for voluntary cancellation, or for any of the following reasons:

(i)  noncompliance with principles,

(ii) noncompliance with post-issuance reporting obligations, and

(iii) other necessary cases brought by investors.

### b.    Registration under the Electronic Securities Act, 2019

Pursuant to the Electronic Securities Act, 2019 securities issued to the public that are to be listed on a KRX market will need to also be registered with KRX, in addition to registration with KSD.

The act prescribes that investors are able to acquire and transfer title, and subsequently exercise any rights stemming from the securities electronically. Consequently, most securities, except those that have effect only in written form (e.g., commercial paper), are subject to mandatory electronic registration. Once registered electronically, securities issued in physical form shall not be in effect any longer.

For details on the Electronic Securities Act, 2019, please refer to Chapter II.C.1.

## I.    Listing of Debt Securities

While the listing of debt securities on KRX has not materially changed since 2018, KRX now features a large segment for sustainable finance instruments under the Korean term for "SRI bonds." However, KRX is considering changing the term "SRI bonds" to "ESG bonds," in line with international best practice.

### 6.    Listing of Socially Responsible Investment Bonds on Korea Exchange [New]

To make the classification and listing process more transparent, and the issuance process easier, KRX issued its SRI Guidelines in 2019. Under the guidelines, SRI bond issuers submit the relevant documents—such as a report on the use of proceeds, impact report, performance report, and external review report—according to the type of bonds. Especially regarding the external review report, SRI bond issuers must establish a bond management framework to be reviewed by an external professional institution to determine whether they comply with established international principles, including those established by the ICMA and the Climate Bonds Initiative.

The listing process itself is not different from the one detailed in the *ASEAN+3 Bond Market Guide Republic of Korea*. At the same time, the KOSPI Market Listing Regulation and the KOSPI Market Disclosure Regulation (i.e., the listing and disclosure rules of KRX) have been updated as recently as March 2024 to allow for a differentiation between conventional and SRI bonds. For information on these changes to the listing and disclosure rules, please refer to Chapter II.J.

By listing SRI bonds as such in the dedicated segment, issuers are exempted from listing fees and annual dues for a period of up to 3 years, in an effort to reduce their funding costs (see Chapter VI.B for details). Investors in turn can quickly establish which bonds are recognized as SRI bonds and access standardized information on the SRI Bonds website of KRX.

# IV

# Bond and Note Transactions and Trading Market Infrastructure

Information in this chapter relates to developments in bond market trading, transactions, and related subjects that have occurred since publication of the *ASEAN+3 Bond Market Guide Republic of Korea* and is presented in the context of the structure used in that bond market guide.

## A.    Trading of Bonds and Notes

**Figure 4.1a: Trading Volume by Bond Type in the Exchange Market, 2018–2023**

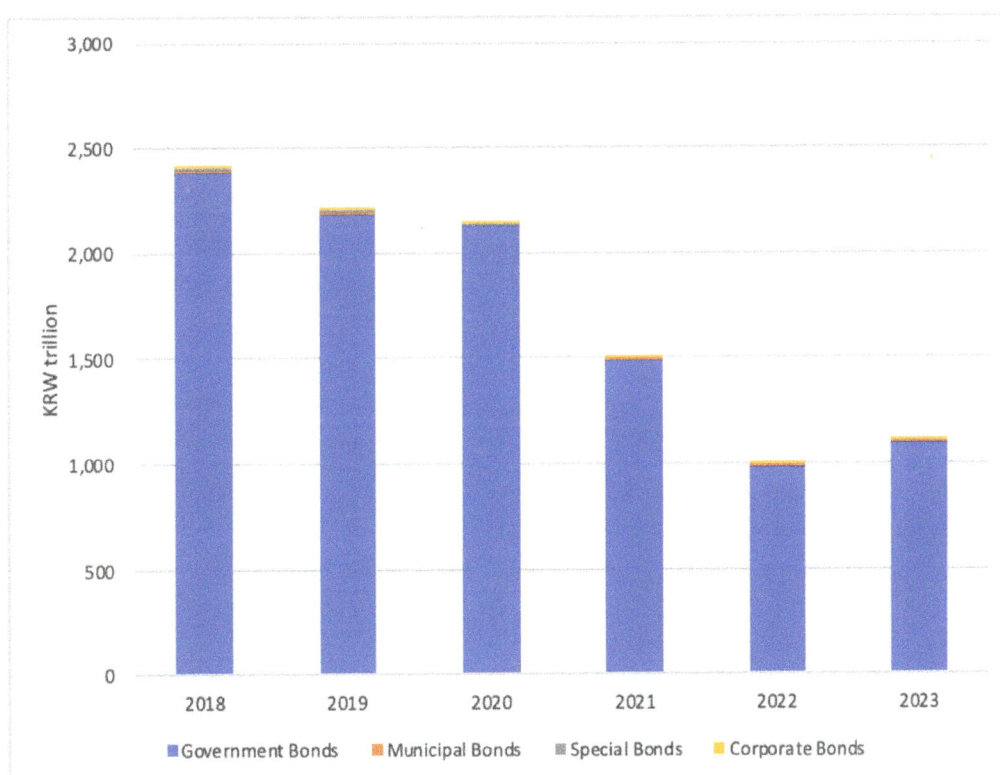

KRW = Korean won.
Note: Data as of December 2023 and include socially responsible investment bonds.
Source: Korea Exchange.

Trading of bonds and notes in the secondary market is conducted on KRX and in the OTC bond market administered by KOFIA. **Figures 4.1a** and **4.1b** provide an update on the trading volume in the exchange and OTC market segments, respectively, since the publication of the original *ASEAN+3 Bond Market Guide Republic of Korea* in 2018.

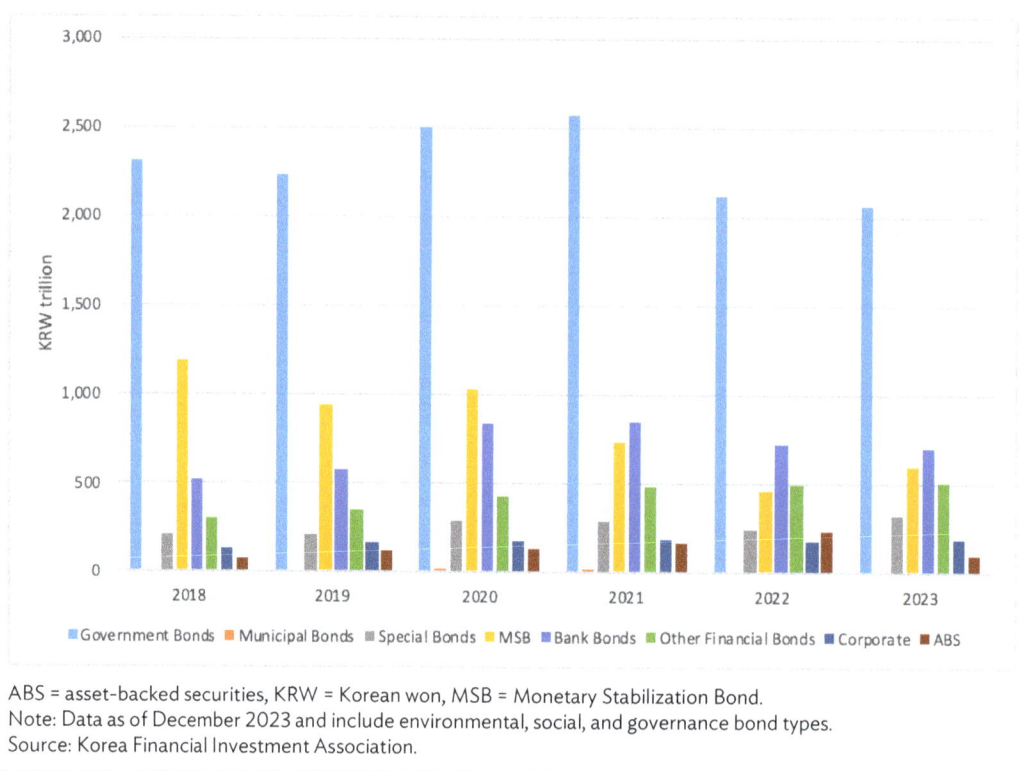

Figure 4.1b: Trading Volume by Bond Type in the Over-the-Counter Market, 2018–2023

ABS = asset-backed securities, KRW = Korean won, MSB = Monetary Stabilization Bond.
Note: Data as of December 2023 and include environmental, social, and governance bond types.
Source: Korea Financial Investment Association.

Trading in KTBs dominates both the exchange and OTC market segments, while trading volumes for other bond types are marginal (in relative terms) on KRX but represent a more sizeable share of the OTC market.

In addition to the data provided by KRX and KOFIA on their websites and in annual publications, comprehensive data on bond market volume and value, bonds outstanding, and breakdowns by instrument type are available from *AsianBondsOnline*.[29]

## F.    Bond Information Services

At the time of publication of the original *ASEAN+3 Bond Market Guide Republic of Korea*, the issuance of sustainable finance instruments had not been evident in the Korean market, as was the case for many markets in the region. This has changed quite significantly in the intervening years. The first issuance of green and social bonds occurred in the Korean market in 2018, and Korean institutions and corporates are now known as prolific issuers of sustainable bonds, including both ESG (or SRI) bonds (see Chapter III.B), both in the domestic and overseas markets.

---

[29] For details, see https://asianbondsonline.adb.org/economy/?economy=KR.

## 5.    Information on Socially Responsible Investment [New]

Socially responsible investment is the terminology used to describe sustainable finance instruments listed on KRX. In relation to the bond market, SRI bonds comprise green bonds, social bonds, sustainability bonds and sustainability-linked bonds, and like instruments.

### Figure 4.8: Korea Exchange's Socially Responsible Investment Bonds Web Page

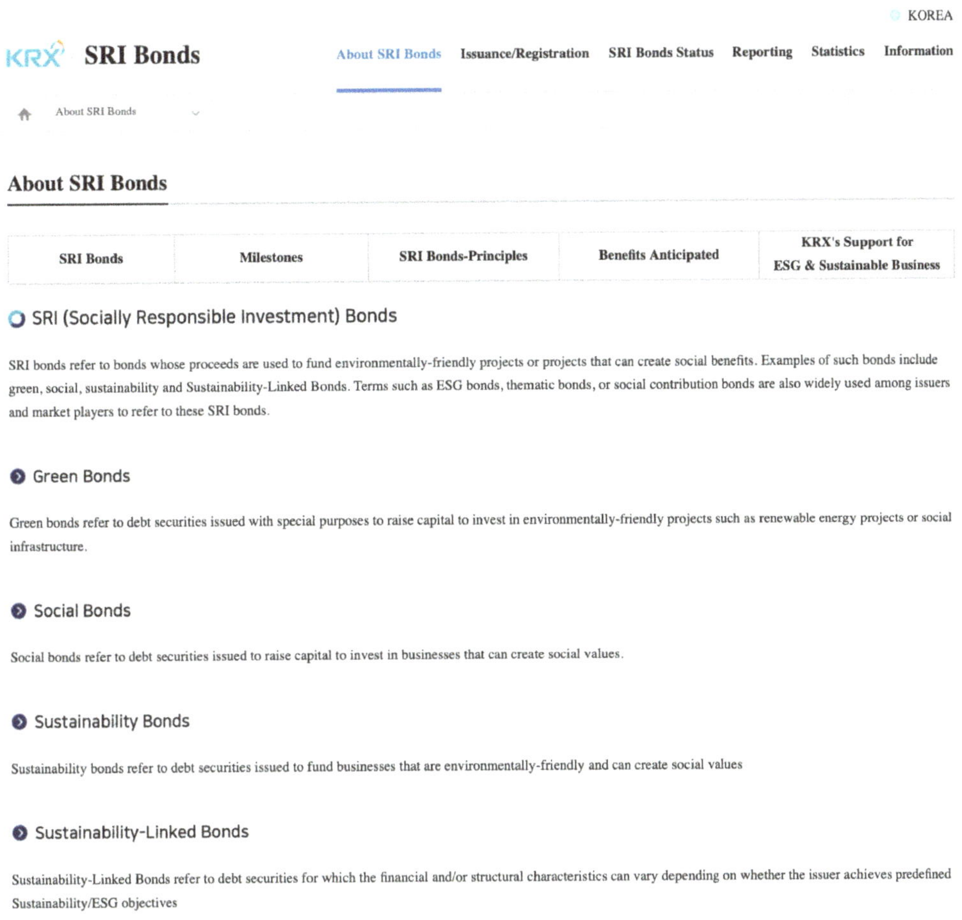

ESG = environmental, sustainable, and governance; KRX = Korea Exchange; SRI = socially responsible investment.
Source: Korea Exchange. SRI Bonds. https://sribond.krx.co.kr/en/01/01010000/SRI01010000.jsp.

At the time of publication of this update note, KRX provided comprehensive information on SRI bonds on dedicated web pages, including descriptions of each instrument type, background information on milestones in the domestic and international markets, the relevant principles, and other related information (**Figure 4.8**). The web pages also describe the issuance of "K-Green Bonds," which are green bonds issued in the Republic of Korea, and compares the issuance process between an SRI bond and a conventional bond.[30]

KRX also offers statistics on the instrument types on these web pages, including listing status and trading data, which may also be downloaded. At the time of publication of this update note, the web page had identified 2,062 issued SRI bonds from 229 separate issuers; all are listed on KRX, with a total issuance size in excess of KRW240 trillion. In fact, all SRI bonds issued in

---

[30] For details, please see https://sribond.krx.co.kr/en/04/04010000/SRI04010000.jsp.

the Republic of Korea are listed on KRX, typically for profiling purposes. Significantly, KRX also offers the relevant issue documentation for download, including underlying bond management framework and external review, if so applicable.

Underlying the KRX activities are the Guidelines for Operation of Segment Dedicated to SRI Bonds, in addition to the general KRX listing rules.[31] For more information on these guidelines, and how they link to the K-Taxonomy and related guidelines from the relevant authorities, please refer to Chapter II.J.2.

## J.    Interest Rate and Fixed-Income Futures

As of the end of 2023, KTB futures with tenors of 3, 5, and 10 years were listed and traded on KRX, having been first listed in 1999, 2003, and 2008, respectively. At the same time, the issuance of longer-tenored KTBs, such as the 30-year KTB, has increased in recent years, reaching 28.5% of total KTB issuance in 2023, which is of particular interest to, for example, insurance companies. Correspondingly, investors (including nonresidents) have increasingly been holding longer-term instruments without being able to cover their portfolios with adequately termed hedging products.

Market watchers have for years argued the need for longer-termed derivatives, preferably exchange-traded for increased transparency, to address the hedging gap in the Korean market in view of evolving portfolio compositions and government issuance patterns.[32]

In a speech during the annual KTB conference in Seoul on 26 October 2022, Deputy Prime Minister and Finance Minister Kyungho Choo announced the introduction of a 30-year KTB futures by the first quarter of 2024, with the MOEF working with KRX and market participants toward such introduction.[33]

KRX began to list the new 30-year KTB futures contracts on 19 February 2024. Trading practices and contract details do not materially differ from those of short-termed KTB futures contracts.

## K.    Critical Benchmark Rates [New]

The Government of the Republic of Korea recognized the need for one or more critical benchmark interest rates in the domestic market, following the declaration that the LIBOR would no longer be serviced as an international benchmark rate effective 1 July 2023. Correspondingly, parliament passed the Act on the Management of Financial Benchmarks of the Republic of Korea in November 2019, which followed the recommendation of the Financial Stability Board to establish relevant domestic reference rates, known as critical benchmark rates, and became effective on 24 November 2020.

To identify and determine relevant benchmark rates, the government established the Benchmark Rate Reform Task Force in June 2019. Its Working Group on Developing an Alternative Benchmark Rate, made up of industry representatives from market institutions and market participants, recommended two critical benchmark candidates that led to the

---

[31] The KRX rules may be found via a separate tab on the SRI Bonds web page at
https://sribond.krx.co.kr/en/05/05040000/SRI05040000.jsp.

[32] Lee, H. 2020. The Necessity to Activate Long-Term ETD in Korea. *Journal of Derivatives and Quantitative Studies: Futures Research*. 28 (3). 149–71. https://doi.org/10.1108/JDQS-08-2020-0020.

[33] From the 9th International Conference on Korea Treasury Bonds. 2022. Era of KTBs Worth KRW1,000 trillion, Challenges and New Leap Forward. 26 October. Seoul.
https://english.moef.go.kr/pc/selectTbPressCenterDtl.do?boardCd=N0001&seq=5439.

appointment of market infrastructure providers to collect relevant data and calculate those benchmarks for the market activities they help facilitate. Details on the critical benchmark rates are provided below (in the order in which they were established).

1. Korea Overnight Financing Repo Rate (Calculated by the Korea Securities Depository)

KOFR represents the critical benchmark rate at which market participants have priced overnight repo transactions in KTBs and MSBs, the most common short-term money market transaction in the Korean domestic market. KOFR is calculated by KSD, with effect from 18 April 2022, since KSD facilitates the domestic repo market in the Republic of Korea. The rate and related information are available—in both Korean and in English—from a dedicated KOFR website operated by KSD (**Figure 4.9**).

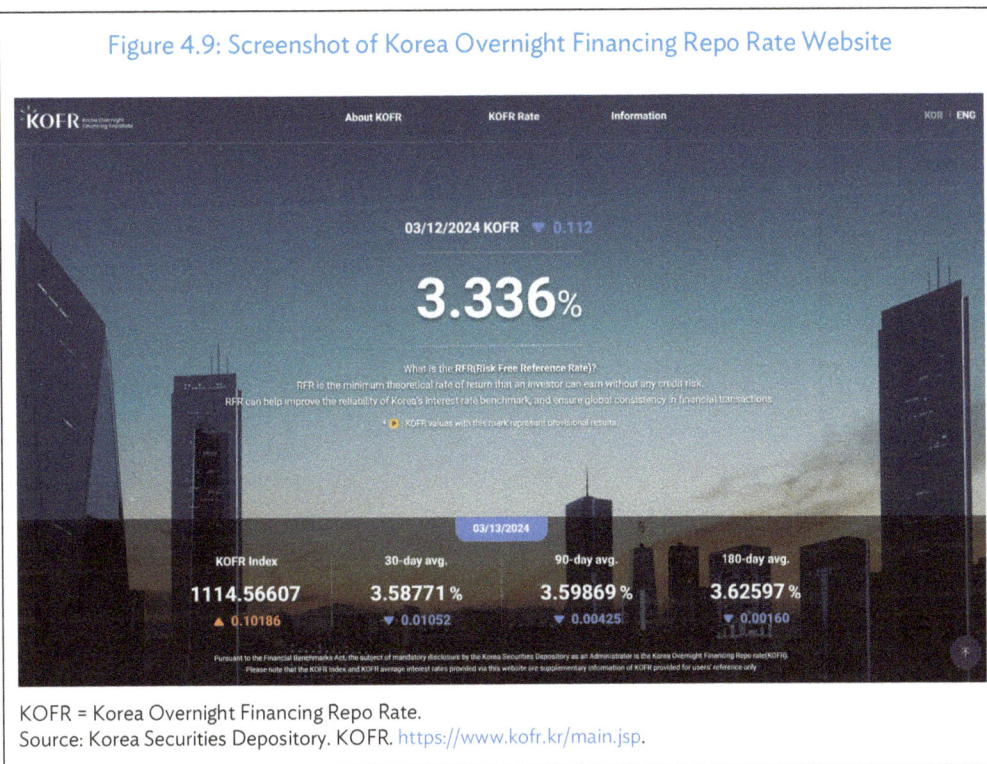

Figure 4.9: Screenshot of Korea Overnight Financing Repo Rate Website

KOFR = Korea Overnight Financing Repo Rate.
Source: Korea Securities Depository. KOFR. https://www.kofr.kr/main.jsp.

2. Certificate of Deposit Rate (Calculated by the Korea Financial Investment Association)

The CD benchmark rate calculated and disclosed by KOFIA, explanatory remarks on the rate and its underlying components, as well as the calculation methodology are all available on the KOFIA Business Information Service website in both the Korean and English languages. KOFIA, which facilitates the OTC market where CDs are traded, has been publishing the CD rate by 4:30 p.m. every business day since 2 October 2023 (**Figure 4.10**).[34]

---

[34] The KOFIA website is available in the English language at https://www.kofiabond.or.kr/index_en.html.

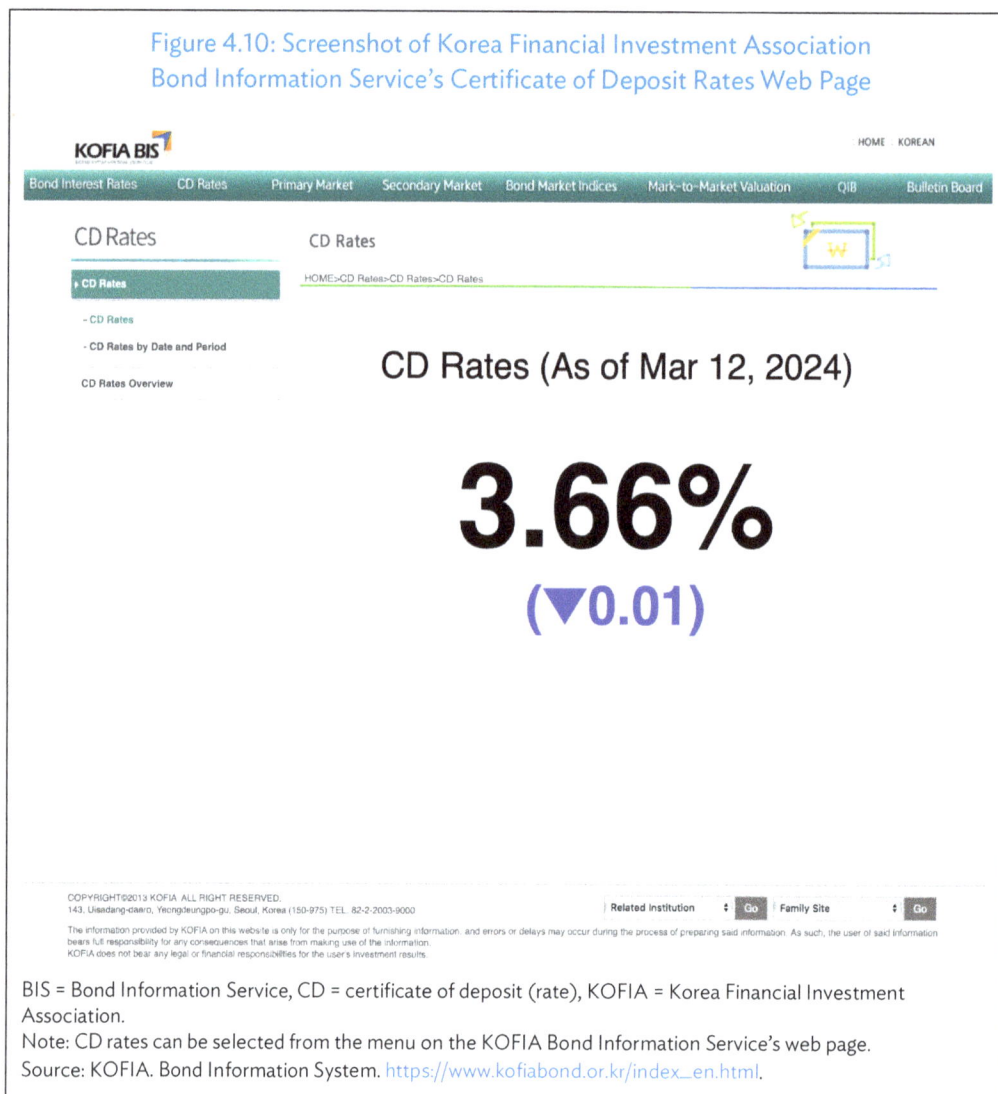

Figure 4.10: Screenshot of Korea Financial Investment Association Bond Information Service's Certificate of Deposit Rates Web Page

BIS = Bond Information Service, CD = certificate of deposit (rate), KOFIA = Korea Financial Investment Association.
Note: CD rates can be selected from the menu on the KOFIA Bond Information Service's web page.
Source: KOFIA. Bond Information System. https://www.kofiabond.or.kr/index_en.html.

The rate takes its name from the underlying CDs issued by AAA-rated domestic banks in the Republic of Korea, in effect offering a representative interest rate at which domestic banks borrow money in the money market. The CD rate is also referenced as "CD91" because the CDs typically have a 91-day tenor, although the rate is calculated on transactions with a tenor of 80–100 days.

# VI

# Bond Market Costs and Taxation

This chapter contains critical updates to taxation practices in the Korean bond market, also focusing on more recent announcements with a bearing on the service costs of certain bonds for issuers. A comprehensive description of bond market costs and other taxation subjects can be found in the original *ASEAN+3 Bond Market Guide Republic of Korea*.

## B.     Listing Fees

This section is included in this update note to detail applicable concessions offered to issuers for the listing of SRI bonds—also referred to as ESG or thematic bonds—on KRX.

### 1.     Listing Review Fee

SRI bonds issued by corporates have been listed on KRX and registered in the dedicated SRI Bonds segment since 2019.

In support of the introduction of SRI bonds, KRX has waived listing review fees (initial listing fees) for new issuances in the SRI Bonds segment since 15 June 2020. This exemption had initially been announced for a duration of 3 years but has since been extended to cover the period until 14 June 2025.

### 2.     Annual Listing Fee

Similarly, KRX has been granting a temporary exemption of annual listing fees for debt securities registered in the SRI Bonds segment until 15 June 2020, covering a 5-year period since the introduction of this concession in 2020.

## C.     Ongoing Costs for Issuers of Corporate Bonds and Notes

The content of this section adds to the original cost items for issuers by offering details on the recently announced support by the Government of the Republic of Korea for interest payments by issuers offering SRI bonds in the Korean bond market.

### 3.     Support for Interest Payments under the K-Taxonomy [New]

Issuers of SRI bonds who list and register their instruments on the dedicated SRI Bonds platform operated by KRX are principally able to avail an interest payment subsidy offered by the MOE under measures supporting the K-Taxonomy (see Chapter III.B for details on the K-Taxonomy).

The incentive is available for large companies at interest rate support of 0.2%, while small and medium-sized enterprise issuers would be able to claim 0.4% support for their payable interest rate. In effect, the MOE would pay the mentioned amount of interest and the eligible issuer would pay the remaining interest rate. However, practically, the issuer would pay interest to bondholders in full and claim the subsidy from the MOE thereafter. The subsidy period per issuer is limited to 1 year (i.e., for the number of interest payments an issuer is liable to pay within 1 year from the approval of the MOE). The calculation of the subsidy follows the market practice for accrued bond interest calculation in the Republic of Korea (i.e., actual/365).

To help incentivize potential issuers of green bonds and test the usefulness of the proposed interest payment scheme, the MOE conducted a trial program in late 2023, in which 23 public and private companies were planning to issue green bonds and obtain the interest payment subsidy, at a cost of approximately KRW5.1 billion.

For more details on the K-Taxonomy, as well as the related industry guidelines, please refer to Chapter III.B.

## H.    Taxation Framework and Requirements

For ease of reference, **Table 6.4** displays the tax rates applicable to nonresidents and foreign corporations with relevance for the bond market at the time of publication of this update note.

Table 6.4: Duties and Taxes on Fixed-Income Securities in the Republic of Korea
(For Nonresidents and Foreign Corporations)

| Duties and Tax | Type of Bond | Tax Rate |
|---|---|---|
| Withholding Tax on Interest Income | Government and MSB | 0%[a] |
| | Corporate | 14%[b] |
| Withholding Tax on Capital Gains | Government and MSB | 0%[a] |
| | Corporate | 10% of transfer value or 20% of gains on the transfer, whichever is lower[c] |
| Stamp Duty | N.A. | N.A. |
| VAT | N.A. | 10% |

MSB = Monetary Stabilization Bond, N.A. = not applicable, VAT = value-added tax.
[a] Following the Ministry of Economy and Finance's announcement in December 2022, with effect from 1 January 2023; applicable principally to KTBs and MSBs, but may be extended to debt instruments issued by public sector entities with additional documentation requirements.
[b] Total tax rate is 15.4% if local tax is included.
[c] Total tax rate is 11% of transfer value or 22% of gains on the transfer, whichever is lower, if local tax is included.
Sources: ASEAN+3 Bond Market Forum constituents and Ministry of Economy and Finance. 2022. Pre-Announcement of Legislation on the Revision of the Enforcement Decree of the Income Tax Act and the Corporate Tax Act. Press Release. 17 October.
https://english.moef.go.kr/pc/selectTbPressCenterDtl.do?boardCd=N0001&seq=5437.

Nonresidents and foreign corporations are subject to taxation on domestic income, but the types of taxation vary based on domestic business location, domestically sourced income, tax treaty status (of the nonresident's or foreign corporation's host economy) with the Republic of Korea, and other factors. Previously, both interest income on bonds and capital gains were subject to taxation for nonresidents and foreign corporations. However, as part of measures to make the Korean bond market—and the domestic capital market at large—more attractive to foreign institutional investors, in 2023 the Government of the Republic of Korea introduced a tax concession on withholding tax for interest payments and capital gains on interest and gains from the holding or trading of Korean government bonds (see revised subsection 9).

### 9.    Tax Exemption for Nonresident Investors

This subsection has been revised to include formal definitions of nonresident (foreign) investors, the details of the recent measure to introduce an exemption from withholding tax for these investors, and information on the practical application of the exemption process.

#### a.    Definition of Nonresident (Foreign) Investor

The domestic tax laws classify foreigner investors as either "nonresidents" under the Income Tax Act or "foreign corporations" under the Corporate Tax Act. "Residents" are defined, under the Income Tax Act, as individuals who have their domicile or place of residence in the Republic of Korea for no less than 183 days in a given year of assessment (i.e., one taxable period). "Foreign corporations" are defined, under the Corporate Tax Act, as corporations that have their headquarters or main office outside of the Republic of Korea.

#### b.    Exemption from Withholding Tax on Interest Income from Government Bonds and Monetary Stabilization Bonds

In a pre-announcement of intended changes to existing legislation on 17 October 2022, the MOEF referenced its intention to create a more conducive investment environment in the Republic of Korea, including changes to withholding tax on interest income and capital gains from investments in KTBs and MSBs;[35] the tax measure was to take effect from tax year 2023.[36]

While the measure, referred to as an exemption from withholding tax for nonresident (foreign) investors and part of a larger strategy to make the Korean capital market more attractive for these investors, was principally available as of 1 January 2023, it only attained the force of law with the actual amendments of the Corporate Tax Act (as well as the Income Tax Act, with relevance for individual investors) effective 1 July 2023. In the meantime, the government treated the withholding tax as zero-rated for any foreign investor wanting to avail the tax concession.

#### c.    Practical Application of Tax Exemption

To be eligible for tax exemption, nonresident (foreign) investors should submit a tax exemption application. In a move to enhance investor-friendly practices in the capital market, an official application form for tax exemption in English has been made available since July 2023, in accordance with the enforcement rules of the Income Tax Act and Corporate Tax Act.[37]

---

[35] The NTS clarified that financial securities, housing bonds, and foreign exchange stabilization bonds also qualify for the tax exemption, as they are considered government bonds.

[36] The pre-announcement by the MOEF can be found at
https://english.moef.go.kr/pc/selectTbPressCenterDtl.do?boardCd=N0001&seq=5437.

[37] In the terminology of the NTS, the application form is referred to as a Non-Taxation Application Form, as referenced in the 2023 Guidance on Non-Taxation of Interest Income/Capital Gains from Investment in Government Bonds/Monetary Stabilization Bonds.

Due to the efforts of market participants in discussions with the NTS, an application for eligibility need only be submitted once to the withholding agent or qualified intermediary; a new form and supporting documents will only need to be submitted if relevant details of the investor change. The key document (the completed application form) may subsequently be shared with other intermediaries in the domestic markets, such as securities firms (brokers) or other withholdings agents. Most likely, custodians will be the party facilitating the process, since they act as standing proxy (i.e., the principal representative for the investor in the Korean market).

### d.    Documentation Requirements

To obtain eligibility for a withholding tax exemption, two key documents must be produced by the investor; in part, these documents may be submitted to the custodian or other intermediary during the account opening process or as part of periodical KYC practices. Documents (here mentioned for a foreign institutional investor not using a "Qualified Foreign Intermediary" [QFI]) include the following:

i.    NTS Application Form for Non-Taxation of Government Bonds (form name is shown as: Application for Tax Exemption on [to tick] Interest Income/Capital Gains from Investment in Government Bonds or Monetary Stabilization Bonds [for Foreign Corporations], or NTS Application Form for Non-Taxation/Tax Exemption on Korean Source Income under the Tax Treaty), or NTS Application Form for Non-Taxation/Tax Exemption on Korean Source Gains from Transfer of Securities under the Tax Treaty; and

ii.    original certificate of residence or a permissible alternative (see subsection f).[38]

Only when the total amount to be exempted exceeds KRW1 billion, and the claim is lodged under a tax treaty, does the foreign investor need to submit additional supporting documents (listed immediately below), other than the certificate of residence and tax form(s), to show that the investor is the real beneficiary of the income source in the Republic of Korea:

(i)    names and addresses of board members;
(ii)    list and details of stockholders and their shareholdings; and
(iii)    audit reports for the past 3 full years, which an investor has submitted to its home market authorities.

These documents need only be submitted once to the custodian or principal contact of the investor, who will then send the information to the NTS as a matter of record. Certificates of residence need only be submitted again if relevant details of the investors change. Investors using the services of a QFI should submit the relevant documents (specific form types apply) to the QFIs (details on QFIs can be found in subsection 11). There is no requirement for formal confirmation from the NTS. The exemption of withholding tax may begin upon completion of the documentation process.[39]

---

[38] For easy reference, tax forms may be downloaded from the NTS English language website at www.nts.go.kr/english/main.do; select "Resources," then "Forms."

[39] Process description and applicable details in part adapted from 2023 Guidance on Non-Taxation of Interest Income/Capital Gains from Investment in Government Bonds/Monetary Stabilization Bonds.

The above information on documentation requirements was believed to be accurate at the time of publication of this update note. Foreign investors, or those with an interest to invest in KTBs and MSBs, and to avail of the tax exemption, should get in touch with their global custodian, ICSD, or broker—or their domestic custodian or securities firm in the Republic of Korea (as the case may be)—for up-to-date documentation requirements and other details.

### e.    Tax Refund

If nonresident investors paid withholding tax but were eligible for the exemption from withholding tax at the time, the investor may submit a request for a tax refund to the withholding agent (e.g., custodian or securities firm) within 5 years of the original tax payment. The withholding agent will file an amended tax return to the NTS for this purpose.

### f.    Documents as Alternatives to Certificate of Residence

Korean authorities recognize the fact that the form, format, and issuers of certificates of residence, certificates of domicile, or similar documents differ greatly depending on the legal and regulatory framework in the home market of an investor. As such, regulatory prescriptions and market practice have resulted in the acceptance of different types of documents in lieu of a certificate of residence, as detailed in **Table 6.5**.

### Table 6.5: Overview of Alternative Documents in Lieu of a Certificate of Residence

| Investor Category | Documents that can Replace a Certificate of Residence |
|---|---|
| Individual | One of the following documents:<br>- copy of passport<br>- identity card or government-issued document with full name and address<br>- Foreign Investor Registration Certificate |
| Corporation | One of the following documents:<br>- Certificate of Registration for Corporation<br>- government-issued document with corporation name and address<br>- Foreign Investor Registration Certificate |
| Government Agency Pension Fund | One of the following documents:<br>- government-issued document or equivalent document that can verify identity of actual investor<br>- Foreign Investor Registration Certificate |
| Overseas Investment Vehicle | (1) In the case of an Overseas Public Investment Vehicle (i.e., a public fund in the economy of establishment) (pursuant to §119-3④, Income Tax Act; §93-3④, Corporate Tax Act)<br><br>One of the following documents that can verify the public fund in the economy of establishment:<br>- fund establishment certificate<br>- fund registration certificate<br>- document issued by supervisory authority<br>- other equivalent document<br><br>*continued on next page* |

continued on next page

Table 6.5 *continued*

(2) In the case of other public funds
    (pursuant to §179-5 of the Enforcement Decree of the Income Tax Act;
    §132-5 of the Enforcement Decree of the Corporate Tax Act)

One of the following documents that can verify the fund's establishment:
- fund establishment certificate
- fund registration certificate, or similar
- Foreign Investor Registration Certificate

Document(s) that can verify that the fund qualifies as an Overseas
Investment Vehicle or Equivalent to an Overseas Public Investment Vehicle

(3) In the case of an Overseas Private Investment Vehicle deemed as the
    Beneficial Owner
    (pursuant to §119-2①, Income Tax Act; §93-2①, Corporate Tax Act)

One of the following documents that can verify the existence of the overseas
investment vehicle:
- fund establishment certificate
- fund registration certificate
- document issued by supervisory authority
- other equivalent document
- Foreign Investor Registration Certificate

(4) Others investment vehicle types
Document(s) as abovementioned that are applicable to ultimate beneficial
investors

Source: Adapted from National Tax Service, Republic of Korea. 2023. *Guidance on Non-Taxation on Interest
Income/Capital Gains from Investment in Government Bonds/Monetary Stabilization Bonds.*
https://www.nts.go.kr/english/na/ntt/selectNttInfo.do?mi=10790&nttSn=1326124.

## 11.    Qualified Financial Intermediary

The QFI concept refers to foreign corporations with headquarters or a main office in an
economy with which the Republic of Korea has entered into a tax treaty. A QFI has to be
approved by the commissioner of the NTS as a corporation conducting business activities
similar to those of KSD and fulfilling the function of a securities custodian. The NTS will
conduct a comprehensive examination of applicants before a decision. QFIs may be global
custodians, ICSDs, or other international intermediaries.

Only QFIs are able to act as withholding agent for foreign investors for tax purposes.
Foreign investors not using a direct relationship with a domestic custodian or other
intermediary will need to submit their tax exemption application, certificate of residence,
and other applicable documents (see subsection 9) to the QFI. Given the nature of the
omnibus accounts, ICSDs offering their clients indirect access to the Korean bond market
will be required to have QFI status.

Both Clearstream and Euroclear have since acquired QFI status (in March 2023 and March
2024, respectively) through the formal approval from the NTS, in time for the
commencement of the indirect market access option (see Chapter II.K and M for details).

# VII

# Market Size and Statistics

The original *ASEAN+3 Bond Market Guide* was published in January 2012 and included several pages of Korean bond market statistics, including historical data such as bond holdings, bondholder distribution, outstanding amounts, and trading volumes. Not surprisingly, these data became stale soon after publication.

Hence, a chapter comprising bond market statistics has been discontinued. In the *ASEAN+3 Bond Market Guide Republic of Korea* published in 2018, this chapter was replaced with a list of recommended sources for detailed, accurate, and current information sources on the Korean bond market. These sources have been updated below in alphabetical order.

- *AsianBondsOnline* (an ASEAN+3 initiative led by the Asian Development Bank)
  https://asianbondsonline.adb.org/korea.php
    - Market-at-a-Glance
    - Data (market size, yields, indicators, ratings, including historical data)
    - Market structure
    - Market summary
    - News (latest statistics)

- Bank of Korea
  https://www.bok.or.kr/eng/main/contents.do?menuNo=400110
    - Treasury & Debt Securities, Overview of Securities Business
    - Payment and Settlement Systems (as downloadable PDFs)

- Korea Exchange
  http://bond.krx.co.kr/main/main.jsp
    - Introduction of KRX bond markets
    - Listing and trading statistics on KRX bond market
    - Issuance information
    - KRX regulations regarding listing, disclosure, and trading
    - Fixed-income indices calculated by KRX (http://enindex.krx.co.kr)
    - International Securities Identification Number information
      (http://isin.krx.co.kr)

- Korea Financial Investment Association
  http://www.kofiabond.or.kr/index_en.html
    - Bond interest rates
    - Primary market information (issuance, maturity statistics)
    - Secondary market information (trading records, turnover, etc.)
    - Bond indexes
    - QIB market (QIB bonds, disclosure documents)
    - Mark-to-market benchmark yields
    - CD rate

# X

# Recent Developments and Future Direction

## A.    Recent Major Developments

Recent major developments are considered those that occurred in the Korean bond market since the publication of the *ASEAN+3 Bond Market Guide Republic of Korea* in May 2018. For easy reference, the developments are reflected in reverse chronological order.

### 1.    Introduction of 30-Year Korea Treasury Bond Futures (2024) [New]

In October 2022, the MOEF announced that it was working with Korea Exchange and market participants toward the introduction of 30-year KTB futures, likely in 2024. At the time of the announcement, the longest-dated hedging instruments traded on KRX were 10-year KTB futures introduced in February 2008.

The planned introduction was in response to a shift toward longer-tenored government bonds being in demand, particularly from insurance companies. In fact, the MOEF stated that 30-year KTB issuance had increased from KRW20.1 trillion to KRW47.8 trillion over the 5-year period to 2021, with KTBs representing 26.5% of total issuance for 2021.[40]

Trading of 30-year KTB futures contracts commenced on 19 February 2024. During the listing ceremony, the MOEF reiterated its commitment to maintaining liquidity in the underlying long-tenored government bonds, including through off-the-run and on-the-run issuance.[41]

### 2.    Introduction of Indirect Market Access for Foreign Investors via an International Central Securities Depository Omnibus Account for Korea Treasury Bond Holdings (2024) [New]

The package of measures to make the Korean capital market more attractive to foreign investors, announced by the MOEF, contained the proposal to make available to foreign investors the option to obtain indirect market access to the Korean bond market through an omnibus account for KTB investments maintained by eligible ICSDs. To make such a proposal feasible, the set of measures also contained the exemption of foreign investors from withholding tax on sovereign debt securities (see subsection 7 in this section).

This account option will require the use of an intermediary who can give foreign investors access to the Korean market and maintain such omnibus accounts on behalf of the investors. Such an intermediary would need to be recognized as a tax processing entity (or QFI) by the NTS and fulfill certain reporting requirements (see also Chapter VI.H).

---

[40] As reported by *Yonhap News Agency*. 2022. S. Korea Seeks to List 30-Year Treasury Futures by 2024. 18 October. https://en.yna.co.kr/view/AEN20221018009800320.

[41] The full MOEF press release on the date of initial listing can be found at https://english.moef.go.kr/pc/selectTbPressCenterDtl.do?boardCd=N0001&seq=5781.

As far back as a 2016 press release, the FSC had acknowledged the challenges stemming from the need for domestic custodians and brokers to maintain segregated accounts for each foreign investor.[42] A subsequent trial of an omnibus account for equities investments in 2017 was not taken up by the market due to the heavy burden of reporting rules, according to an FSC press release on 13 December 2023. However, with the IRC system recently abolished, the market can make another attempt to establish an account structure considered best practice in many other capital markets.

The new account option would allow foreign investors to access Korean sovereign bonds without entering into a proxy agreement with a custodian in the Korean market and needing to maintain securities and cash accounts in the domestic market. In effect, the omnibus account of ICSDs becomes an indirect market entry option for foreign investors.

The first parties to avail themselves of the new omnibus account option were ICSDs Clearstream and Euroclear. Both parties signed memoranda of understanding with KSD at the end of 2022 and have since been working out contractual and operational details. KSD will maintain the intermediaries' omnibus account in addition to segregated accounts. The service is expected to be available from the first half of 2024 and the FSS was in the progress of determining the form and contents of transaction reporting by ICSDs.

Since this option is applicable only to foreign investors, a comprehensive description of the new account option, related process(es), as well as procedural challenges can be found in Chapter II.M.

### 3.    Mandatory English Disclosure (2024) [New]

In April 2023, the FSC announced the introduction of mandatory disclosure of material information in the English language for issuers that are stock-listed on KRX, as part of its efforts to make the Korean capital market more attractive for nonresident investors.[43]

The FSC, together with the FSS and KRX as executing agencies of this policy measure, are pursuing a phased approach, starting with large, listed companies from 2024 and expanding the requirement to all remaining listed companies from 2026. In a first for the bond market, issuers stock-listed on KRX with bonds outstanding (regardless of the market of issuance) will have to include company information in English in any disclosure related to these bonds. The disclosure obligations continue to follow the existing prescriptions in the FSCMA as well as the disclosure rules issued by KRX.

Details of the disclosure provisions and the proposed timetable can be found in Chapter II.G.

### 4.    Liberalization of the Onshore Foreign Exchange Market (2023) [New]

The MOEF, together with the BOK, announced in February 2023 that the trading hours of the onshore interbank FX market will be significantly extended. Consequently, the onshore interbank foreign exchange market has been operating from 9 a.m. to 2 a.m. the following day, effective 4 October 2023, instead of closing at 3:30 p.m., which had been in line with KRX trading hours. The new trading hours effectively align with the closing of the London interbank market and will also allow the inclusion of transactions executed after 3:30 p.m. in market benchmark rates.

---

[42] For details on the FSC's review of the challenges for the Republic of Korea's market at the time, please refer to the 2016 press release at https://www.fsc.go.kr/eng/pr010101/22123.

[43] Information in this update note in part based on an FSC press release, which is available at https://www.fsc.go.kr/eng/pr010101/79726?srchCtgry=&curPage=&srchKey=sj&srchText=&srchBeginDt=2023-04-01&srchEndDt=2023-04-30.

The policy measure by the MOEF was part of the larger strategy to improve the attractiveness of the Korean capital market (see also other sections in this chapter) and followed much industry feedback on the challenges stemming from an early closing time for investors and intermediaries situated in other time zones. These challenges included market access generally as well as incurring trading premiums in after-hours trading.[44]

More information on these liberalization measures can be found in Chapter II.M. Please also see the proposed future changes to FX market participation, as detailed in section B of this chapter.

### 5.    Replacement of Investor Registration Certificate with Legal Entity Identifier (2023) [New]

On 25 January 2023, the FSC announced that the IRC, the investor access concept for the Korean capital market, would be abolished. The announcement represented a key cornerstone of the government's efforts to further open and liberalize the Korean capital market, and came in response to much investor and industry feedback in recent years. At the same time, the IRC's abolition is part of a set of measures to make the capital market more attractive to foreign investors (see also other topics in this section).

Foreign institutional investors wishing to access the Korean market for the first time no longer require approval from the FSS but would need to provide to intermediaries in the Korean market their LEI to serve as investor identification, in addition to market-typical account opening documentation; an individual investor would use her or his passport details accordingly. The use of LEI is practical since most institutional investors are increasingly required to provide their LEI as counterparty identification when participating in major financial markets or market segments globally.[45]

The policy change was approved at a cabinet meeting on 5 June 2023 and took effect on 14 December 2023. A detailed review of this development and its implications can be found in Chapter II.K and Chapter II.M.

### 6.    Exemption of Foreign Institutional Investors from Withholding Tax (2023) [New]

As part of its policy measures to make the Korean market more accessible and attractive for foreign investors, the Government of the Republic of Korea announced in December 2022 that foreign investors would be exempted from withholding tax on income and capital gains from their investment in KTBs and MSBs. A withholding tax exemption is also possible for other public debt instruments, and additional documentation may apply for certain amount thresholds; specific application forms, documentation requirements, and application practices apply.

In a positive sign of streamlining the exemption process, the necessary application form and relevant supporting documents will only need to be submitted once and may be shared among market intermediaries (brokers and custodians) that service a foreign investor. This practical solution was achieved by continuous discussions between the NTS and securities industry participants. The exemption of withholding tax became effective on 1 January 2023, in line with a new fiscal year in the Republic of Korea.

---

[44] Compiled from market authorities' press releases, other public domain sources, and legal commentary, including Kim & Chang. 2023. *Insights Newsletter*. 13 February. https://www.kimchang.com/en/insights/detail.kc?sch_section=4&idx=26745.

[45] For more information on the LEI and how it is used in other markets, please see https://www.gleif.org/en.

Details on the exemption, relevant forms, application process and documentation requirements, and relevant procedural descriptions can be found in Chapter VI.H.9.

### 7. Review and Enactment of Digital Assets Legal Framework (2022–2023) [New]

On 17 August 2022, the FSC announced the formation of a private–public joint task force to review existing laws and regulations, and to propose the necessary components of a legal framework suitable for digital assets. Part of the strategy to achieve this is the creation of the so-called Digital Asset Basic Act as fundamental legislation, while amending existing key legislation—such as the Financial Investment Services and Capital Markets Act—with references to that act or supplementary provisions. The framework is intended to cover crypto-assets, digital securities, as well as the tokenization of any assets.

Previously, the only law featuring any form of definition of digital assets had been the Act on Reporting and Using Specified Financial Transaction Information, commonly known as the AML Act, which became effective in March 2021. While the Electronic Securities Act, 2019 had been enacted prior to this initiative, it was found to be a valuable foundation for a digital assets framework as it already contained important key features of securities, such as the existence purely as an electronic (digital) record. Here, the formal definition of securities tokens is envisaged.

As a first step toward the envisaged legal framework, the Act on the Protection of Virtual Asset Users was passed into law on 18 June 2023; it will become effective on 1 July 2024, allowing market participants to adjust their activities or services according to new provisions.

The completion of the legislative work on the digital assets framework is expected for 2024, with laws typically becoming effective 1 year after promulgation.

For more details on the digital assets framework, particularly the definition of digital or virtual assets, please see Chapter III.A.

### 8. Introduction of the K-Taxonomy, K-Taxonomy Guidelines, and Green Bond Guidelines (2021–2023) [New]

The MOE announced the K-Taxonomy on 30 December 2021, as a policy framework that stipulates principles and standards for green economic activities and measures to encourage such activities. At that time, the MOE also publicized the K-Taxonomy Guidelines in an effort to pre-empt greenwashing and help accelerate capital flows into green activities. The MOE and the FSC, together with KRX, published in late 2020 the K-GBG, which was intended as the first official guidance to the market on green bonds, their definition, and related practices.

The K-Taxonomy and supporting policy measures took effect from 2023. The MOE initially conducted a pilot phase in the financial and other sectors from April to November 2022 to test market applicability. The pilot phase saw six companies issue green bonds for green energy generation and zero-emission vehicle infrastructure, in conjunction with the MOE, to the tune of KRW640 billion.

Since 2023, the MOE has been providing financial incentives for the issuance of green bonds. Incentives under the K-Taxonomy and K-GBG consist of support for interest coupon payments and extend from bonds to green asset-backed securities, but they do not cover support for issuance costs.[46]

For more detailed information on the K-Taxonomy, the K-Taxonomy Guidelines, the K-GBG, and sustainable finance instruments, please refer to Chapter III.B. The financial incentives offered to potential issuers of green bonds are further detailed in Chapter VI.C.

### 9.    Development of Critical Benchmark Rates (2019–2023) [New]

With the discontinuation of the LIBOR as the benchmark interest rate for global markets, and the subsequent drive for regulatory authorities to determine an alternative benchmark rate for each market, the Government of the Republic of Korea legislated the need to develop multiple critical benchmark rates in the Act on the Management of Financial Benchmarks of the Republic of Korea, promulgated in November 2019 and effective on 27 November 2020. The act sets out standards for determining such critical benchmarks for the administrators and the administration of such benchmarks, as well as the obligations of the users of these critical benchmarks.[47] Consequently, two major reference rate candidates were developed by authorities.

Authorities had set up a Benchmark Rate Reform Task Force in June 2019 to determine a risk-free reference rate similar to the ones being established in major financial markets to replace LIBOR. The task force included representatives from the BOK, FSC, the Korea Capital Market Institute and Korea Federation of Banks, KOFIA, KRX, and KSD. The work of the task force, through its Working Group on Developing an Alternative Benchmark Rate, resulted in the formulation of the Korea Overnight Financing Repo Rate (KOFR) as a critical benchmark. KOFR is being calculated based on overnight repo transactions on sovereign debt instruments (KTBs and MSBs), a common practice also employed in other markets and, hence, considered a risk-free reference rate. KSD was designated to act as the KOFR-calculating agent in November 2021 since it facilitates the domestic repo market. The publication of KOFR officially commenced on 18 April 2022.[48]

In parallel, the FSC designated (in 2021) the domestic CD rate as one of the important critical benchmark rates for the Korean market. In local market terms, the rate is also referred to as "CD91," reflecting the typical 91-day tenor of the underling products. In June 2023, the FSC appointed KOFIA as administrator of the CD rate, owing to its role as facilitator for the domestic OTC market. KOFIA commenced its role as CD rate calculator with effect from 2 October 2023.[49]

---

[46] The K-Taxonomy and Green Bond Guidelines are available from the MOE website at https://www.me.go.kr/skin/doc.html?fn=20230831172157.pdf&rs=/upload_private/preview/. In addition to an official version in English, many law firms and other service providers offer English translations and interpretations of the provisions, typically on a sector or industry basis. The information in this note is partly based on an MOE press release available at https://www.korea.net/Government/Briefing-Room/Press-Releases/view?articleId=1568510&insttCode=A260112&type=N.

[47] Interested parties can view the full text of the act in English via the Korea Law Translation Center at https://elaw.klri.re.kr/eng_mobile/viewer.do?hseq=56616&type=part&key=23.

[48] For more information on KOFR's and KSD's role as calculating agent, please see https://www.kofr.kr/main.jsp.

[49] For more information, please see FSC. 2023. CD Rate as Critical Benchmark Rate to Take Effect from October 2. Press Release. 25 September. https://www.fsc.go.kr/eng/pr010101/80823?srchCtgry=&curPage=&srchKey=&srchText=&srchBeginDt=&srchEndDt=#:~:text=In%20March%202021%2C%20the%20FSC,benchmark%20rate%20in%20June%202023. The CD rate itself is published on the Korean version of the KOFIA OTC market website at https://www.kofiabond.or.kr/.

10.     Introduction of Non-Competitive Bids Option for Government Bonds
        (2019–2021) [New]

Announced by the MOEF as part of measures to revitalize the government bond market in 2019, the introduction of non-competitive bids for government bonds was intended to ensure stability in the primary market and comes with incentives for primary dealers to regularly underwrite new issues.

A corresponding revision of the Regulations on KTB Issuance and Primary Dealer Operation for this so-called "non-competitive underwriting system" placed more weight on underwriting obligations of primary dealers than their market-making obligations by giving additional points for underwriting toward the quarterly evaluation of primary market participants. In addition, a fourth non-competitive bid option was introduced in 2021.

Please also see Chapter III.E. for an explanation of the additional non-competitive bid option.

11.     Issuance of Green Bonds and Other Sustainable Finance Bonds (2013–2022)
        [New]

The first domestic green bond was issued by the Korea Development Bank in 2018, which also issued the first domestic social bond in the same year. Also, in 2018, the Export–Import Bank of Korea issued the first sustainability bond in the local market.[50]

The term used in the Korean market for such instruments is socially responsible investment bonds, typically referred to as SRI bonds and also tracked on KRX by this designation. SRI bonds comprise green, social, sustainability, and sustainability-linked instruments, and are understood to be synonymous with thematic bonds.

In the international market, the Export–Import Bank of Korea issued the first green bond in 2013. The first Climate Bonds Initiative-certified green bond was issued in April 2022 by Shinhan Bank.

Details of SRI bonds and their typical features in the Korean market can be found in Chapter III.B, while Chapter IV.F contains further details on SRI bond information services provided by KRX.

## B.     Future Direction

This section summarizes developments that are envisaged in the next 12–18 months, either based on existing announcements or market feedback. For practicality, these future developments are organized in chronological order.

---

[50] Text is based in part of information about SRI bonds on the KRX website, which acts as the key information resource for such instruments in the Korean market, available at https://sribond.krx.co.kr/en/01/01010000/SRI01010000.jsp.

1.      Further Measures to Liberalize the Onshore Foreign Exchange Market (2024) [New]

As an additional policy measure under what the MOEF termed "Improvement Measures for Foreign Exchange Market Structure" in its February 2023 announcement, foreign financial institutions would in the future be able to participate directly in the domestic FX market—without having to establish a local entity in the Republic of Korea or having to use a domestic FX bank of broker to transact on their behalf. The measure refers to RFIs; details and conditions are further explained in Chapter II.M.[51]

The foreign exchange market reform measures will be officially implemented during the second half of 2024 after 6 months of pilot operation.

2.      Inclusion of Korean Government Bonds into Global Bond Indexes (2024) [New]

The Government of the Republic of Korea is anticipating the inclusion of Korean sovereign bonds in the FTSE Russell World Global Bond Index in the near future. Index provider FTSE Russell had added the Republic of Korea to its watch list in September 2022, following announcements by the government that it would address some of the structural issues in the Korean bond market that had been highlighted by the industry.

An inclusion in the World Global Bond Index would result in significant extra investment in KTB and MSB by domestic and foreign investors in an effort to balance global bond portfolios that are tracking the index.

According to media reports, it may take up to 2 years for designated markets to move from the watch list to an actual inclusion in the index. The next update to the World Global Bond Index is scheduled for March 2024.[52]

---

[51] Adapted from MOEF. 2023. Improvement Measures for Foreign Exchange Market Structure. Press Release. 6 March. https://english.moef.go.kr/pc/selectTbPressCenterDtl.do?boardCd=N0001&seq=5509.

[52] An example is *Korea Times*. 2023. Korea Fails To Be Included on FTSE Russell's Global Bond Index. 30 September. https://www.koreatimes.co.kr/www/biz/2023/10/602_360222.html.

# Appendix 2
# Practical References

For easy reference and access to further information about the topics discussed in this update note, interested parties are encouraged to utilize the following links (all websites are available in English); items marked "[New]" were not included in the *ASEAN+3 Bond Market Guide Republic of Korea* or have since changed.

AsianBondsOnline (Asian Development Bank)
https://asianbondsonline.adb.org/economy/?economy=KR [New]

Bank of Korea
http://www.bok.or.kr/eng/main/main.do

Financial Services Commission [New]
https://www.fsc.go.kr/eng/index

Financial Supervisory Service
https://www.fss.or.kr/eng/main/main.do?menuNo=400000

Korea Exchange (KRX)
https://global.krx.co.kr/main/main.jsp
KRX Regulations
https://global.krx.co.kr/contents/GLB/06/0601/0601000000/GLB0601000000.jsp
KRX listed socially responsible investment bonds [New]
https://sribond.krx.co.kr/en/01/01010000/SRI01010000.jsp

Korea Financial Investment Association (KOFIA)
http://eng.kofia.or.kr/index.do
KOFIA Regulations
http://eng.kofia.or.kr/brd/m_15/list.do
KOFIA-calculated CD Rate [New]
https://www.kofiabond.or.kr/index_en.html

Korea Securities Depository (KSD)
https://www.ksd.or.kr/en
KSD Regulations
https://www.ksd.or.kr/en/resource-center/news-and-regulations/regulations
KSD-calculated Korea Overnight Financing Repo Rate [New]
https://www.kofr.kr/main.jsp

Ministry of Economy and Finance [New]
https://english.moef.go.kr

Ministry of Justice [New]
https://www.moj.go.kr/moj_eng/index.do

Ministry of the Environment [New]
https://eng.me.go.kr/eng/web/main.do

# Appendix 4
# Glossary of Technical Terms

This glossary focuses on terms that appear in this update note. Terms marked with [New] appear in this update note for the first time.

| | |
|---|---|
| Account Management Institution | Participant at Korea Securities Depository (KSD), effectively a custodian for securities on behalf of customers or own holdings |
| authorized institutions | Licensed banks, restricted license banks, and deposit-taking companies as defined in the Banking Ordinance |
| big data | high-volume, high-velocity and/or high-variety information assets that demand cost-effective, innovative forms of information processing that enable enhanced insight, decision-making, and process automation (according to Gartner, Inc. IT glossary) [New] |
| CD rate | Candidate critical benchmark rate, calculated by Korea Financial Investment Association (KOFIA), which is based on interest rates of certificates of deposit (CDs) with a 91-day maturity issued by AAA-rated commercial banks [New] |
| CD91 | Refers to a CD with a typical tenor of 91 days [New] |
| critical benchmark rate | Designation in the Republic of Korea for market reference rate [New] |
| disclosure | Activities by the issuer or appointed intermediaries to furnish investors with financial information on the issuer, its activities, and relevant developments |
| disclosure requirements | Prescription of disclosure obligations for issuers by regulatory authorities or trading market operators in law or regulations |
| electronic securities | Term used in law and regulations in the Republic of Korea for securities maintained purely in the form of electronic records [New] |
| electronic securities system | Term used, instead of "depository," in law and regulations in the Republic of Korea for a system that records electronic securities only [New] |
| enforcement | Term widely used in the context of the Korean market to describe the validity or effectiveness of a law or regulation [New] |
| enforcement date | Term widely used in context of the Korean market and in general discourse to express the effective date of a law or regulation [New] |
| ESG bonds | Typical designation for bonds aimed at creating economic, social, or governance value; the term is primarily used by KOFIA [New] |
| financial investment business | Summary term for entities carrying out activities in the capital market under authorization by and oversight of the Financial Services Commission (FSC) |

| | |
|---|---|
| green bond | In the Republic of Korea, a bond that supports green activities defined under the K-Taxonomy [New] |
| guideline(s) | Nonbinding document issued by a regulatory authority or market institution with the purpose to aid the interpretation and/or practical application of provisions in law and regulations [New] |
| Investor Registration Certificate | Official market-entry registration for nonresident investors to access the Korean capital market (until 14 December 2023) |
| Korea Green Bond Guidelines | Document issued jointly by the Ministry of Environment and FSC to guide market participants on the issuance of thematic bonds under the K-Taxonomy [New] |
| Korea Overnight Financing Repo rate | Critical benchmark rate calculated by KSD, denoted as the risk-free reference rate for the Republic of Korea, and based on actual overnight repo transactions between financial institutions [New] |
| Korea Treasury Bond | Government bond issued by the Republic of Korea |
| KSD member | Following the introduction of the Electronic Securities Act, 2019 and the designation of KSD as an electronic register, the new name for what was previously a "depository participant" [New] |
| K-Green Bonds | Green bonds issued under guidelines and practices in the Republic of Korea [New] |
| K-Taxonomy | Lays out clear principles and criteria for genuine green economic activities in the Republic of Korea [New] |
| K-Taxonomy Guidelines | Guideline for the interpretation of the K-Taxonomy and application of green economic activities to the financial market [New] |
| listing | Typically, action of submitting a bond issue or other securities to an exchange for the purpose of trading, price finding, disclosure, or profiling |
| Local Operating Unit | Entity issuing the Legal Entity Identifier [New] |
| Monetary Stabilization Bond | Key, often longer-tenored, instrument in Bank of Korea's open market operation to steer market liquidity; classified as a government bond |
| non-competitive bid | Options of participation in Korea Treasury Bond auctions by, for example, individual investors or those allowing the Ministry of Economy and Finance to fulfill its issuance target beyond competitive auctions |
| omnibus account | Represents the ability to keep the assets of multiple investors in a single securities account [New] |
| over-the-counter | transaction platform where buyers and sellers directly interact and trade based on offer and acceptance or negotiation |
| place of disclosure | Marketplace or designated entity where updated disclosure information of an issuer is to be submitted and/or posted |
| profile listing | Listing without intention or expectation of trading, for purposes of disclosure or to reach a wider investor universe [New] |

| | |
|---|---|
| Qualified Foreign Intermediary | Nonresident financial institution appointed by the National Tax Service to act as withholding agent for tax to be paid by foreign investors [New] |
| Qualified Institutional Buyer | Professional investor concept in the Korean bond market |
| QIB Market | Bond market where the bonds and note issued by private placement are traded among Qualified Institutional Buyers (QIB) |
| QIB Market–debt securities | Bonds and notes that are eligible to trade on the QIB Market |
| registration | Refers to the act of registering a bond with KOFIA as a prerequisite to be tradeable in the over-the-counter market |
| registration | Now also refers to the act of registering a socially responsible investment (SRI) bond in the designated SRI Bonds market segment on KRX; activity is separate from and in addition to listing [New] |
| segregated account | Account structure where each investor maintains their own named account or accounts |
| self-regulatory organization | Association or market institution empowered by law or regulatory authorities to govern a market or market segment, administer members, and set and enforce market rules |
| social bond | Debt securities issued to raise capital to invest in businesses that can create social values (according to KRX) [New] |
| socially responsible investment bonds | Term specific to the Korean market for bonds aimed at creating environmental, social, and governance value; the term is actively used by KRX and has been adopted by market stakeholders [New] |
| SRI bonds | Korean term for sustainable finance instruments in the form or bonds or notes [New] |
| SRI Bonds | Dedicated segment on Korea Exchange for the listing of and disclosure in relation to SRI bonds [New] |
| SRI Guidelines | Document issued by KRX to guide market participants in the classification of sustainable finance instruments and practices [New] |
| standing proxy | Role of the custodian or securities firm as official representative of a foreign investor in the Korean market [New] |
| sustainability bond | Debt securities issued to fund businesses that are environmentally friendly and can create social values (according to KRX) [New] |
| sustainability-linked bond | Debt securities for which the financial and/or structural characteristics can vary depending on whether the issuer achieves predefined sustainability objectives (according to KRX) [New] |
| third-party FX | The ability for an investor to choose a foreign exchange transaction provider other than their appointed custodian [New] |
| virtual assets | Definition of asset types that only exist in digital form, part of digital assets classification [New] |

Source: ASEAN+3 Bond Market Forum.

www.ingramcontent.com/pod-product-compliance
Lightning Source LLC
Chambersburg PA
CBHW050053220326
41599CB00045B/7394